MORE ADVAN...
SUBV...

"In *Subversia*, D.R. Haney reveals his life as a series of vivid episodes—formative and destructive, hilarious and heartbreaking—that illuminate the mind of an intense soul whose charisma is outshined only by his unrelenting honesty."

— Richard Cox
Author of *Rift* and *The God Particle*

"D.R. Haney does in his essays what I thought now virtually impossible: he describes contemporary reality. I've known D.R. for about a quarter century, and this is a quality that he always has in conversation; as his many friends will attest, talk is not so much a cure (per Freud) as a voyage. In these essays he has made the transition (or translation) of that voyage not just to the page but to Literature."

— George Porcari
Author of *A Stroll in the Park: Photography and* Blow-Up

"Only D.R. Haney, one of the literary-minded lost of Generation X, teetering on the edge of insanity and brilliance, could slam together *Subversia*, a peculiar, albeit engrossing, set of American experiences."

— Nick Belardes
Author of *Lords* and *Random Obsessions*

"The man writes a book. It is a great book of fiction. How will I ever top this? he says. He walks around, and sits and thinks. Then he writes a great book of essays."

— Ben Loory
Author of *Stories for Nighttime and Some for the Day*

SUBVERSIA

A COLLECTION OF PIECES FROM
THE NERVOUS BREAKDOWN

D.R. HANEY

Published by The Nervous Breakdown Books
Los Angeles, California
www.thenervousbreakdown.com

First Edition, September 2010
Copyright © 2009, 2010 D.R. Haney

Book Design: Charlotte Howard, CKH Design

Photo Editing: Jeannie Hart

Design, programming and distribution for all digital editions:
    Joseph Matheny of Hukilau.us

The views expressed in this book are those of the author
and do not necessarily reflect those of the publisher.

ISBN 978-0-9828598-0-3

Printed in the United States of America

FOR KERRY

CONTENTS

IV. FAMA

V. LIBER

PREFACE: BRAD LISTI

WHEN I THINK of Los Angeles, I think of Duke Haney. He has lived so many of its lives.

The other day, Duke and I met to discuss this book, the first published by The Nervous Breakdown imprint. We went for a coffee in Hollywood and took a table on the sidewalk, facing Sunset. Across the street: Amoeba Music. One of the last great record stores in L.A., and maybe anywhere. This is the stretch of Sunset, the exact intersection, where Duke almost died in 1990.

"Right over there," he said, pointing. "Right there in front of the store."

Leveled by an oncoming car.

"I remember lying on the pavement, deep in shock. Instinctively, I know I'm in bad shape, but I can't feel anything yet. Then the sun goes away and I look up and see a homeless guy standing over me. And you know what he says? He says, 'Damn, man. Your leg is *bad*.'"

Duke's arm was bad, too. A lot of things were bad.

A lot of things changed after that.

Subversia isn't *about* the accident – not explicitly, anyway – but it was born in that moment, much the same way that *Banned for Life*, Duke's novel, was born in that moment. That's how I see it, anyway. That's how I make it make sense.

I mentioned this to Duke as we sat there, drinking coffee, and he nodded. Then, as if on cue, came the blaring of sirens, and both of us looked left. A police escort was rolling toward us, heading west down Sunset at a crawl. Traffic had stopped in all directions.

It was a pack of joggers. The cops had cleared the way so the joggers could run along the road. Strained faces. Dripping sweat. All were wearing matching T-shirts. Ceremonial. The guy in the lead was holding something.

He was carrying the torch for the Special Olympics.

A couple of onlookers honked their horns in support. The joggers gave a wave, and on they went. Slowly, the sirens faded, and slowly, the traffic resumed. Duke and I continued staring blankly at the boulevard, and for a while we didn't say anything.

Then Duke started laughing a bit. Shook his head and rubbed his eyes. "What do you think God is trying to tell me?" he said.

I told him I had no idea.

— Los Angeles
June 2010

FOREWORD: GREG OLEAR

DARYL REID HANEY posted his first piece at The Nervous Breakdown–"Ice Cream, Heroin, and a Chance Encounter at Ralph's," a vignette on his brush with the doomed indie rocker Elliott Smith–on April 19, 2009, three months after my own (clumsy) entrance onto the TNB stage. Little did I suspect that within a matter of weeks we'd become friends, and that a year later I would have the honor of writing this introduction.

In hindsight, a few things stand out about "Chance Encounter." First, it garnered a mere twenty-nine comments from eleven measly commentators, which, for those of you unfamiliar with TNB's comment culture, is sort of like a new James Cameron film playing in just eleven theaters and selling only twenty-nine tickets. Second, most of the eleven commentators refer to him, clunkily, as "D.R." They were not yet hip to his street name, a sobriquet acquired after the car accident that left him with a John Wayne-like gait, and one befitting of the TNB royalty he would become: Duke.

I was not among the ground-floor eleven, however, because I didn't read the piece. I don't remember why. Probably I was put off by the word *heroin*. I was still new at TNB, still figuring out the personalities of the various writers, not sure yet what to make of it all. I dismissed this Haney character as one of those hepcats who extol their drug experiences. *Look at me! I did smack! Isn't that rad, dude?* Yawn yawn.

It was not until "Norman Mailer and the Shape of My Nose," six weeks and as many entries later, that I finally gave Haney a read. From the gate, I recognized that this guy was something special. His deft handling of the Al Pacino story—I won't spoil it for you, but I will add that Pacino is 5′7″ in platform heels and Duke is a legit 6′2″—was a particular highlight.

My newfound appreciation of Haney's work was fortuitously timed. Two posts after my conversion to fandom—by now I'd read through his archive—Duke posted "And a New Chapter Begins," concerning the release of *Banned for Life*, a labor-of-love novel that took him nine years to complete. At the end of the piece, Duke posts a photo of his friend TJ Nordaker kissing a copy of the book. *I don't have any fucking words,* went TJ's caption, *so I took this picture.*

"Okay, then," I thought. "If a grown man likes a book so much he's moved to take a photograph of himself smooching it like it's a fucking teddy bear, perhaps this is something worth investigating."

I bought myself a copy of *Banned*, and soon discovered that TJ's reaction was entirely appropriate. I found myself glancing at the blurbs on the back cover—all positive, of course, but focusing too much on the milieu of punk rock and not enough on the quality of the writing—and becoming irked that they were not sufficiently glowing. Then I realized that, with my own novel on its way into the world, I could furnish my own blurb, which I promptly did:

Banned for Life is about punk rock? Sure, just like *Moby-Dick* is about whales. This is the thrilling story of Jason Maddox, '80s musician turned '90s screenwriter, who embarks on an Ahab-like quest of his own–although the blubbery object of his fascination is a vanished punk-poet. Like Melville, D.R. Haney has created a world so rich in detail, so authentic, so damned cool, you want to take up a harpoon–or, in this case, a guitar–and join the fray. *Banned for Life* is literary fiction at its best–funny, heartbreaking, hopeful, and every bit as inspiring as the punk music it extols.

See what I did there? I compared Duke to Herman Melville, author of perhaps the Great American Novel. In my view, *Banned* is a book for the ages. Had it been delivered into the world in hardcover, by an august house–if Farrar, Straus, and Giroux, say, had given it the Franzen treatment–Duke would be well on his way to establishing himself as the first literary rock star of the new century. I firmly believe that. He has all the requisite ingredients: the talent, the charisma, the gravitas, the cool. He even has groupies (virtual groupies, but still). All that's missing is the renown.

Like a punk band on the cusp of making the big time–think Die Princess Die in "Have You Seen My Head?"–Duke is now known only to the cognoscenti. For the time being, he is ours and ours alone. Will he break up like Die Princess Die, or blow up like the Ramones? I've got my money on the latter. The collection you're about to enjoy comprises Exhibit A. From the ranks of America's most celebrated writers, D.R. Haney will not be banned for life.

The best epitaph a man can gain is to have
accomplished daring deeds of valor against
the enmity of fiends during his lifetime.

"The Seafarer"

I. MEMORIA

I WAS A CHILD PORN MODEL

WHEN I WAS TEN, my parents sent me to summer camp for two weeks. They made the arrangements secretly, knowing a fit was inevitable the minute they broke the news. I was an explosive kid, coming as I did from a histrionic family, and my parents wanted me gone for a while so they could rage at each other without me around to upstage them.

In any case, they announced at the last minute that I was campbound, and I characteristically threw a fit, to no avail. The camp, for boys only, was located somewhere in the Appalachians and administered by the Elks Lodge. Boys from all over the state of Virginia were attending, and it must have been a big deal, since, the morning I left, a photographer from my hometown paper materialized to snap a picture of me and twelve or so others awaiting deportation in the Elks Lodge parking lot. One kid cried. I frankly felt like joining him, never having been separated from my family for more than a couple of days, but I swallowed my tears, afraid of appearing as pathetic as the crybaby. Besides, I didn't want to give my parents the satisfaction. I was still pissed at them for their ambush. Even so, I hugged them just before I was packed in a car by an Elk and shuttled to the gulag.

Well, of course it wasn't nearly as bad as anticipated. I enjoyed the camp, in fact. I met a real live Jew, and, as a Southern Baptist, I was able to interrogate him as to why his people had crucified Christ. I listened to Jimi Hendrix for the first time, and perused the counselors' girlie magazines, hoping to catch one of them banging a chick in the woods, as rumor said they did. Still, I never got to see any chicks getting banged, just as I never got bit by a timber rattlesnake, which was something of a goal at the time. Not that I sought the pain involved; I just thought a rattlesnake bite would make for a great story. Plus, I wanted to be a herpetologist. Adults would stare at me with bugged-out eyes when I mentioned that. They'd say, "You want to be a *what*? I don't even know what that *is*."

I was a brilliant child. Everybody always said so. The sky was the limit, people said. Instead I became a writer.

But the best thing about that camp was its heavy emphasis on American Indians: their crafts and ceremonies and so on. I was obsessed with American Indians. I read every book I could about them. I had favorite tribes, changing preferences based on new information about methods of warfare, or because unbiased study revealed the Crow pompadour as infinitely superior to the Blackfoot bangs. The camp counselors were wowed by how much I knew about Indians, and they singled me out to Bobby, the camp director.

Bobby was probably in his early fifties. In memory, he looks like the director John Huston: white haired and rope thin, with a perpetual, lupine smile. He was the oldest person at the camp by far, and everyone there looked up to him; during meals, his table was unfailingly crowded with campers and counselors who hung on his every word. We'd ask, for instance, if he believed in Bigfoot, and he'd say, "Well, I'm certainly open-minded about the subject. I mean, the gorilla wasn't discovered till the turn of the century. And I've seen the photos of Yeti footprints taken on Mount Everest, and to me they look authentic. So it's possible Bigfoot is related to the Yeti."

And so on. Bobby was intelligent and a lay scholar when it came to Indians. I soon became his protégé: the shining light of the Indian Club, to which half the kids at camp belonged. I was even allowed to try on his one-hundred-year-old Lakota war bonnet, with its crown of eagle feathers and ermine tails that dangled from beaded medallions. No other kid could touch that thing, just as no other kid could leave the camp; but one night Bobby drove me to his mother's house–he lived there with her in the off-season–to show me his collection of arrowheads and pre-Columbian pottery fragments. He let me pick out a fragment to keep. I didn't realize he had an agenda. My parents were concerned about pedophiles, as parents invariably are, but any fear they had was expressed to me in the usual admonitions: *Don't accept rides from strangers*, and so on. And Bobby wasn't a stranger. On the contrary, I regarded him as a friend, not to mention a mentor.

But Bobby liked naked boys. Games were played in which we disrobed. For instance, we had a water-balloon fight, in which the camp was divided into two teams–red and blue–and, running around in loincloths, we splattered each other with balloons filled with red and blue paint. Bobby photographed the fight, which was innocent enough, but afterward he shot us skinny-dipping as we washed off the paint. We thought it was funny. We posed for him, mugging. Even the counselors, who were almost all in their late teens, posed and played along. No one, I'm sure, suspected Bobby's motives. Child porn hadn't yet become a hot-button topic, and a respectable organization like the Elks Lodge couldn't possibly place a pedophile in charge of two hundred boys.

"Oh, yeah, that's funny stuff, Buzz. Hold it right there."

Click.

The two weeks passed much too fast, and they climaxed with a public presentation of Indian dances, mostly performed by the counselors, who knew their stuff. One could do the hoop dance: a perennial favorite at powwows. Loinclothed campers served as extras, and one would be chosen for the star spot: the dance at the end of the show. I don't remember the name of the dance, which wasn't truly a dance at all, and may not have been traditional, but it went like this: a slain warrior is woken by the Great Spirit, who beckons him with waving arms to the happy hunting ground. The Great Spirit, wearing Bobby's Lakota war bonnet, was painted white from head and toe – by Bobby. There was never any doubt as to which boy would play the Great Spirit. I had a lock on the part.

The night of the presentation, I went as scheduled to Bobby's cabin, accompanied by friends from the Indian Club, though I was the only one allowed inside. Bobby had the paint ready. He was also ready with his camera. He wanted to take some "before" pictures, he said, which struck me as logical and part of the fun, so I took off my clothes and stood naked before him as he snapped the shutter. He didn't ask me to pose provocatively. I'm sure he'd long since determined just how far he could push things.

Then he painted me. I don't remember if he used a brush or his hands, but there was no fondling or lingering, though he painted my privates along with everything else. Then, after the paint had dried, I put on a loincloth, as well as the war bonnet and tassels that hung from my wrists and thighs, and walked outside for my friends to admire me. Jokes were made – "Man, you're whiter than Casper!" – but I knew they thought I looked badass. A tipi had been set up in the woods near the presentation site as a makeshift greenroom, and I had to be sneaked inside it so the crowd wouldn't see me, since my appearance was meant to startle. I remained in the tipi till the close of the show, and the number went off as practiced, though the war bonnet, designed for a grown man, was weighty and hard to balance. Then I returned to Bobby's cabin, where he photographed me in the shower.

I left the camp the next day, driven home by a gruff Elk, and maybe two weeks later a letter from Bobby arrived. Enclosed were photos of the dance, but none of me naked, of course. Even so, my mother was aghast at the sight of me dressed only in a loincloth. I thought she was being ridiculous. I was an *Indian*, Mom. That's what Indians *wore*. Don't you know *anything*?

In fact, I think she did. I never returned to the Elks Lodge camp. Instead, for the next few years, I was sent to a Christian camp in North Carolina, where my body held no interest for people so bent on controlling my mind.

GRAND ILLUSIONS

MY FAMILY HAS been in Virginia since the seventeenth century, and many in my line were farmers, including my grandparents on both sides. I was especially close to my maternal grandparents and spent a lot of time on their dairy farm, which my grandfather designated Grand View after the land, and the house on it, was passed to him by his mother, Della. Her mean streak, legendarily Medusa-like, was not unjustified. Her husband, Hugh, was a circuit rider – that is, a traveling preacher who spread the Gospel on horseback – whose later, untreatable madness may have been triggered by the sudden death of their young daughter, Sara. Another shock was the murder, by a jealous ex, of my beloved great-aunt Nicie's intended as he left the house one night.

The house, which sits at the crest of a hill that does indeed afford a grand view, already had a painful history. It was built in the 1830s by slaves owned by the prosaically named Cowherd family (Della and Hugh acquired the property at the turn of the twentieth century), and during the Civil War there was a skirmish between Yanks and Rebs at the foot of the hill, with part of the house razed by cannonfire. My great-great-uncle Billy, uninvolved in that fight, was an officer in the Confederate Army, and was buried in uniform, as per his request on his old-age

deathbed. He strongly resembled Robert E. Lee in the only photo I saw
of him: white bearded and stately atop a white steed, his riding coat looking Confederate gray in the sepia-toned photo.

This is all to say that family lore uniquely prepared me for the novels
of William Faulkner, with Grand View filling in for many of Faulkner's
Yoknapatawpha County settings. There was, for instance, a gray-wood
shack next to the chicken yard, where I pictured Joanna Burden of *Light
in August* living as a pariah. There was a smokehouse, sweetly smelling of
sultry ham, in the backyard, where I pictured Ringo and Bayard of *The
Unvanquished* playing war. As for the late-night fight of *Absalom, Absalom!*, I transposed that to my grandfather's former horse stable – "former"
because he renounced horses after he was forced to put down an injured
favorite. Of all Faulkner's books, *Absalom, Absalom!* has for me special
resonance, since I read it at Grand View during a summer retreat from
New York. Then, too, it solidified my love of paragraph-long sentences
and pages-long paragraphs.

But my love for Faulkner began with our introduction, *The Sound
and the Fury*, which he wrote under the influence of Joyce, and so fused
stream-of-consciousness modernism with Hawthornian gothic. It was,
I think, the most ambitious novel I'd read to date (I was twenty), and
I naturally saw it taking place at Grand View, with Caddy Compson,
whose soiled underpants so jolted her three damaged brothers, climbing
the mimosa tree that, as a child, I used to climb.

Faulkner spent his final years as writer-in-residence at the University of Virginia, and his grandsons owned a bar in my hometown. Once,
when I was at the bar with my father, the owners both appeared, one of
them a dead ringer for Faulkner in his thirties, and I had an impulse to
walk up to him and say, "I am your grandfather's heir." I was working on
a novel at the time, and later, after I junked it, I wondered at the weird

urge to announce myself as Faulkner's heir—to his grandson, no less. It was youthful hubris, of course, but still, I'd never been so sure of myself, and now it seemed I'd never start another novel, having been so battered by the one abandoned.

I was wrong. I did start, as well as finish, another novel, though the subject matter—punk rock—proves, as if proof were necessary, that I'm not Faulkner's heir. But it was a grand illusion for the second it lasted.

THE DARK UNDONE

THE THOUGHT CAME to me when I was fifteen and trying to sleep on New Year's Eve. Nothing I recall had happened to incite it. I'd spent the night babysitting my younger siblings while my mother attended a party, and she returned home around one in the morning, and everyone went to bed. (My parents had divorced a few years prior, though they continued to quarrel as if married.) My brother was sleeping in the bunk below mine, and as I stared at the ceiling and listened to the house settle, I thought: "Why don't you go into the kitchen and get a knife and stab your family to death?"

It wasn't an impulse; it was a kind of philosophical question that I found myself pursuing. I thought of true-crime cases and wondered at the difference between, say, Charles Manson and me. Why was he capable of killing? Why was I not? Was it a matter of morality? But for me morality was tied to religion, and I'd declared myself an atheist a year or so before. Nor did man's law amount to an automatic deterrent. Some killings – those sanctioned or even performed by the state – were viewed as "right." But wasn't a life a life? So, if I *wanted* to get a knife and stab my family to death, as I knew I didn't, why would that be any more "wrong" than a soldier killing in combat? Because my family was "innocent"? But weren't many victims of war likewise innocent? And why was I wondering in the first place? Didn't serial killers similarly brood before acting? I knew some did. I'd read the letters they sent to the press and police: *Stop me before I kill again. I don't want to do it, but I must.* And maybe I was one of them. Maybe there was no difference between me and Charles Manson. You can't choose what you are; you simply *are*.

I tossed and turned. The quiet of the sleeping house was loud—how loud was the quiet that followed murder? Maybe I was destined to know. I desperately wanted proof—irrefutable proof—that I would never hurt anyone as, more by the minute, it seemed inevitable. My interest in warfare and horror movies and birds of prey now made sense. I was nauseous with fear.

Though years would pass before I heard the term, I was having a panic attack. I also had obsessive-compulsive disorder. Not that I performed the compulsions: repeatedly washing my hands or counting my steps. No, I suffered from what's now known as pure obsessional OCD, commonly referred to as Pure O: morbid, or in any case unacceptable, ruminations "cleansed" by still more ruminations. The subconscious logic is homeopathic—like treated with like—and I was afraid I was going to kill, so, over the next several months, I would dwell on murder when the fear came over me, repelling action with appalling thought.

Welcome to hell.

I AVOIDED KNIVES, and if forced to use one, I would hold it limply afterward like a rat by the tail and quickly discard it. I refused to see any movies or watch any TV shows potentially featuring violence, including comedies. So it was with books. Once, for an English class, I was assigned to read Flannery O'Connor's "A Good Man Is Hard to Find," about a Southern family on a road trip, and it struck me as the funniest story ever—until the family encountered The Misfit, an escaped convict who killed them one by one. I naturally saw myself as The Misfit, and, socially speaking, I *was* a misfit. I favored crowds over intimate settings, thinking crowds would keep my "urges" in check; but even then I might spot a pretty girl and picture myself killing her, knowing that lust and murder are synonymous to a certain kind of homicidal mind.

I confessed my thoughts to my parents. They were dismissive, familiar with my tendency to exaggerate, though my mother was concerned enough to seek out a therapist. He proved passive and useless, but there was a psychologist at my school, Mr. Hughs, who helped me considerably. I saw him for an hour every week in lieu of attending class, and he assured me that I wasn't a Manson in the making. I didn't believe him. I knew little about Manson at the time, but he was the most famous killer in America (though he never technically killed anyone), so I'd fixed on him as my prototype.

"But you're nothing *like* Manson," Mr. Hughs repeatedly told me. "You're an exceptionally smart, talented young man."

"And don't you think Manson is smart? I mean, why can't you be smart and a killer, too? It happens, right? It's *got* to."

On and on it went: me trying to talk Mr. Hughs into confirming the worst. Finally, one day, in the middle of a session, he stood, exasperated, and reached for a diagnostic tome.

"This is Charles Manson," he announced, reading aloud a profile of a psychotic personality type. I don't remember what the type was called, but I instantly knew it didn't apply to me. Of course, I might still be a killer of another type, but Mr. Hughs told me something else that somewhat set me at ease: he was counseling a teacher who'd been troubled by thoughts of killing his family. But they were just *thoughts*, Mr. Hughs emphasized. *Everyone* has strange thoughts, including those of murder.

The obsession began to lift, replaced by others. I had "cancer" on numerous occasions. I was "manic-depressive" and "borderline"; and only slowly did I realize that my real problem was OCD, which no therapist, including Mr. Hughs, ever identified, since, again, I didn't manifest the compulsions.

And then, years later, my initial obsession briefly returned.

I WAS LIVING in L.A. by then, and conducting another round of my long affair with a married woman I'll call Anne. We'd met in New York, and I was friendly with her husband, but I lusted for Anne as she did for me, so we fooled around and stopped, and started again when I was back in New York for an extended stay. I felt guilty about the affair and returned to L.A. thinking it was over, but Anne followed me, telling her husband she was visiting friends. She'd obviously fallen for me, and her behavior seemed increasingly proprietary, with her insistence on serving me, as if trying to force a sense of debt, sulking or crying when I didn't respond as desired. I was younger than Anne, whose intensity rattled me, though it did make for pyrotechnics in the bedroom.

One night, as I was driving Anne to a bar in Hollywood where she'd arranged to meet friends, I pictured myself clubbing her with a tire iron that was lying on the floor of the car. Somebody had broken into the car that day, smashing a window; and the Santa Ana winds were blowing, causing traffic lights and palm trees to sway eerily; and Anne was sulking in the passenger seat, as she'd been sulking before at my house. All of this contributed to a fraught frame of mind, and the thought of attacking Anne triggered memories of similar thoughts at fifteen, and I was suddenly sure I must be a killer after all. I imagined Anne's murder in gruesome detail, afterward dumping her body like the Hillside Strangler, an L.A. serial killer who'd surely driven, victim in tow, on this very stretch when the Santa Anas were blowing.

I was trying to scare myself, of course, as I had at fifteen, treating like with like, which sparked a panic attack made worse by the silence in the car and Anne's ignorance of my ruminations. I sweated and struggled to breathe, my pulse racing, until finally I did the unthinkable.

"Anne," I said, as calmly as possible, "I have to tell you something: I just thought about killing you."

Yes, I admitted it, but she wasn't distressed. She'd always been interested in psychology, especially of the abnormal sort, and her curiosity trumped her fear. She asked me a series of questions as if conducting an intake session, probing my childhood and drawing connections between this event and that one. We talked raptly until the very second we greeted her friends, somehow acting normally with them and resuming our talk the second we left the bar. I'd never been so forthcoming with anyone, including Mr. Hughs, and Anne was equally forthcoming with me. It continued for hours, both of us sharing our darkest thoughts, even in bed, where we seemed to melt into one another when the talk gave way to sex. I'd always thought fucking was fast and hard and making love was slow and gentle, but I was wrong, as I learned that night. In fact, before then, I'd never made love, since I'd never been truly naked. That was the difference: shedding all that hid my heart and exposing it to touch and light.

FOREVER STRANGERS

I PASSED THEM, as I've by now passed millions, and I shared only the briefest of moments in their company. In some cases, we never exchanged a word. Yet I still find myself thinking about these people: extras and bit players in the movie of my life, as I am, or was, in theirs.

■ A hooker, standing on the steps of a fleabag hotel in midtown Manhattan. Her lower lip has all but been cut off, one end of it hanging from a corner of her mouth like a die-hard leech. A cop is beside her, and I've just been mugged a few blocks away, and, still shaken, I try to tell the cop about the mugging. "I can't do anything about it right now!" he barks. The hooker's teeth are chattering, and she moans, "Oh my God, oh my God," again and again, still able to talk, despite not having, for all intents and purposes, a lower lip.

■ A group of teenaged girls sitting on the hoods of cars on an oceanfront strip in Virginia Beach. I'm sixteen and visiting the beach with friends, and as I walk past the girls, I hear one of them say, *"He's* cute." I've never previously heard myself described that way by a stranger. Later, during the same trip, a man in a car pulls up alongside me as I'm walking alone, and says, "Want me to suck your cock?" Which is also a kind of compliment, even though I freak out and say, "No!" My first proposition by an adult, not including those who molested me as a child, and they didn't ask for permission.

▪ A guy in his early twenties, a bit of a hipster, paused on the sidewalk on New York's St. Mark's Place, about to light a cigar. The pretty girl paused beside him is looking on in admiration. I understand. This is before cigars have become a rediscovered nationwide trend, and this kid is doing what I've never seen a guy my age do. It impresses me as the coolest thing ever, because it's so old-school, so traditionally masculine in a way that arty young guys in New York are discouraged from being. I soon become a cigar smoker, as do most of my friends, and when we light up at parties, other guys come up to us and say, "Wow, you're smoking cigars! That's the coolest thing ever!" So I jokingly take credit for the trend to come, though for me it dates to that cool-as-fuck kid on St. Mark's Place, who reminds me, as he walks away with his adoring date, of Robert Doisneau's famous photograph of the kiss outside the Hotel de Ville in Paris.

▪ A woman in her late twenties or early thirties, hitchhiking along the side of Interstate Whatever in the middle of the night, somewhere in the Arizona desert. As she's fully illuminated by the headlights of the car in which I'm a passenger – the only car on the road – I see that she's crying. The woman at the wheel, with whom I'm having a cross-country affair, keeps driving. Yet all the way to L.A., which I'm about to visit for the first time, we talk about the hitchhiking woman, wondering how she came to be in such dire circumstances, both of us wracked with guilt for failing to stop.

▪ An obviously deranged homeless woman in a late-night New York subway station, having an imaginary conversation on a pay phone. "What do you mean, you *reign supreme*?!" she shrieks. "*Nobody* reigns supreme!" Then she hangs up in a huff and pushes her shopping cart down the platform.

▪ A distant figure, which may be male or may be female, in the small park near the Roman Coliseum. It's a hot day in July, and I'm lying shirtless under a tree to cool off. Then I see this figure raise a camera and snap a picture of me. Why? Because I must look like an iconic Roman youth, so at ease in my native city that I'm lying in the shade half-naked near the Coliseum, as I've surely done numerous times before. But I'm a tourist, and so, I assume, is the photographer.

▪ The body of a man under a white sheet on a sidewalk in Hollywood. The sheet doesn't entirely cover his feet or hands. A line of black blood (yes, it's *black*) is trailing from the hidden head. A wrecked motorcycle is overturned nearby. Cops are at the scene, and traffic is stalled, and rubberneckers, including me, strain to see the cause. Somewhere, I think, someone is waiting for this guy, unaware that he's dead. But I know he's dead, and I don't even know his name.

▪ Two men and a woman, all in their sixties, in a battered car on the New Jersey Turnpike, stuck in traffic on an overcast September day. It's the day I'm moving to New York, and I'm stuck in a nearby lane, with my few possessions in a cardboard box beside me. All three people in the battered car have gray skin, matching their gray or white hair. All three look thoroughly used up. Yet to me there's something beautiful about them, because they've been used up by NYC, or at least its immediate surroundings. That's how in love with the city I am: even its human husks seem beautiful.

▪ A girl in her early twenties, buying a box of candy at a kiosk in the center of Belgrade. She has peachy skin, honey-colored hair, gold-flecked eyes. She's with a female friend, who's likewise buying a box of candy. It's maybe midnight, and it seems to me that she and her friend are on their way to a party. I'm too awestruck to approach her. I buy whatever it is I've come to buy at the kiosk, then return to my nearby flat. Three minutes later, I'm kicking myself for not having said anything, and I rush downstairs and dash all around the center of town trying to find her. I never do.

▪ Another beautiful Eastern European girl, this one in Budapest. She's working at an American Express office at the train station, and a good-looking guy, possibly her boyfriend, is standing at the window talking to her. It's a snowy night in December, and I've been stranded with next to no money by a friend (now a former friend), and I desperately need to call a friend in America to ask if he can wire me something so that I can get home to Belgrade. But I don't have a cell phone, and I don't have enough money to buy a card that will allow me to call an operator from a pay phone, and I explain the situation to the girl through the window at the American Express office; and without a pause, she gives me, free, a calling card. A half hour later, $200 arrives, and I eat my first meal in a day or so—a gyro sandwich—as snow falls thickly around me. I love you still, you beautiful Hungarian. I hope you went on to marry that guy, who seemed no less sympathetic, and you now have a flat full of children. The world needs more of your kind.

THE UNINVITED

LATE ONE NIGHT five years ago, as I was revising my novel, *Banned for Life*, I heard a sound: a slight thump, as if a matchbox had fallen to the floor. I stopped typing. Everything was very quiet. I resumed work.

Then, the following night, I heard another sound: this one louder. It seemed to come from the bathroom, which I checked, and, finding nothing amiss, I briefly wondered if my apartment was haunted.

I lived at the time, and still do, in a Spanish-style bungalow built during World War I in a part of Echo Park that served as the backlot for a movie studio owned by Tom Mix, a cowboy star of the silent era. The link to film history is significant. I'm sure I'm not alone in finding old photographs eerie, especially photographs of people long dead; and movies, of course, are individual photographs that, run in sequence, give the illusion of movement, with actors eternally repeating the same actions, just as ghosts are said to repeat the same actions: the hitchhiking girl who seeks a ride to the prom; the decapitated man who seeks his head. Los Angeles, meanwhile, is probably the most photographed city ever, given the countless movies shot there, so in that way it's inhabited by more than its fair share of ghosts. I don't see L.A. as the sunny, seedy, superficial place others do; I see it as haunted.

Not that I literally believe in hauntings—or do I? I've heard a few credible stories, including some from people I know. My neighbors Joe and Heather, for example, who aren't superstitious types, both claim to have seen a ghost peering through their window. Others claim to have seen it, and I was present when one of them gave an account, and I rule out the power of suggestion in his case, since he chided Joe for failing to warn him about the ghost. And now, as I say, I briefly wondered if I had a ghost of my own.

Or maybe it was a mouse. I once had a problem with mice when I lived in New York, though I couldn't remember them making sounds as loud as the one I'd just heard.

I searched the apartment. The only mouse I saw was attached to my computer. I sat again to write and heard another sound. It was well after midnight, but I called my on-off girlfriend Kerry, knowing that, as a writer herself, she'd be awake. Besides, she'd called me more than once to report strange sounds. She was convinced, for a period, that a man was on her roof, though she couldn't explain why he kept returning. I mean, if he planned to rape, rob, and kill her—and she knew he did—why didn't he rape, rob, and kill her the first time he scaled her roof? Kerry's neurosis was one of the reasons for our frequent breakups. Yet, even though she expected me to tolerate her neurosis, she was impatient with mine. I told her about the sounds I'd heard, and, yawning, she said, "It's probably a mouse."

"Yeah, but this sound—it's louder than a mouse would make. I wonder if a cat somehow wandered in here."

I heard another sound, from the darkened kitchen now and, walking toward it, saw the silhouette of a huge rat that was strolling nonchalantly across the tiled floor. It wasn't the size of a New York subway rat—those things are rodent Godzillas—but it was nonetheless big.

"Oh my God!" I said. "Oh my God, it's a rat!"

"Well, now you know," Kerry said, bored.

"What do I do?! How do I get rid of it?!"

"How should *I* know?"

Bitch. I'm going to remember that the next time you call about a man on your roof. I was clueless as to how the rat had gotten inside my place, but two things were clear: it had taken up residence, since I'd now heard it two nights in a row, and it was going to die. Oh, yes. Rats bite. They spread disease. They breed, and soon you're overrun with rats, who likewise bite and spread disease.

My first thought was to starve the rat to death by trapping it in a ground-level cupboard full of pots and pans. Starvation is, needless to say, a slow, cruel way to go, but it didn't require that I kill the rat physically, as I was loath to do. Plus, poison, for instance, could also take a while, and the rat would be free the entire time, possibly to wake me to complain about a stomachache and ask for a Tums.

My second thought was a variation on the first: I could trap the rat in the cupboard and buy some poison and put that inside the cupboard, and the rat would be quarantined, and I could feel better about myself for not having starved it to death. Of course, death by poison is hardly humane, but I was only willing to grapple with ethics to a certain point. I armed myself with a broom and opened the cupboard door, and once the rat, fleeing the broom, made for the cupboard: slam! Welcome to your cruel end, rat! Now I just had to find the bloody thing and let the chase begin.

In fact, it was a chase. I saw the rat and charged with the broom, but the rat refused to accept its cruel end, instead running in every direction except toward the cupboard. It repeatedly ran in my direction, and I flashed on stories I'd heard of rats scurrying up pant legs and snacking on the family jewels. I abandoned the chase long enough to tuck the cuffs of my pants inside my socks and, angry as I hadn't been before, tried to swat the rat, to hopefully kill or stun it, but the damned thing was too fast. At one point it disappeared through a tiny opening beneath the sink, which I couldn't believe, knowing nothing about the flexible skeletons of rats. With labor and patience, I managed to flush it out, and, running forward and stepping back whenever it came near me, I slammed the broom again and again, until finally the rat sought asylum in the cupboard. I slammed the door. That's right, fucker. Your cruel end is on its way.

I'd recently lost my car, which had been impounded by the city for unpaid parking tickets, and my bike had been stolen when I left it unguarded for a second by the cash register at Pioneer Market. So I had to walk, at three in the morning, to a twenty-four-hour drugstore a good distance away, much of it uphill, and, after buying the poison, trek home. But it was worth it. I poured pellets of greenish-blue poison into a small dish and, opening and shutting the cupboard door with Road Runner speed, slid the dish inside. Now I could write in peace.

I heard munching. *Bon appétit, vermin!* But the munching was too loud for the rat to be eating the poison. No, it was chewing the wood of the cupboard door. You never figured on that, did you, genius? You never, as you were devising this scheme, considered that your cupboard is made of fucking wood, did you?

I felt like a character in a Poe story as I listened to the rat munch, munch, munch, slowly chewing its way to freedom. Stop! Make the sound stop! I ran to the cupboard and threw open the door and rammed the broom inside, and the rat darted past me and again disappeared down the tiny opening beneath the sink.

It was almost dawn. I was exhausted. Maybe, I thought, if I leave my back door ajar, the rat will leave while I sleep. It certainly had to know it wasn't welcome, that in fact there was a deranged human intent on killing it.

But it was an obstinate rat. That night I saw it brazenly sitting on the arm of my sofa.

I couldn't call my landlords. We'd sparred since I signed the lease, and I knew they'd find a way to blame *me* for the rat. I walked again to the drugstore, where I bought traps, which I baited with peanut butter, waiting as I wrote for the sound of a trap being sprung. There was no such sound, and the next night I saw the rat again.

I walked up the street to my neighbors Joe and Heather, the ones with the haunted house, and told them about my feeble attempts at extermination.

"Oh," Joe said, "I know how to take care of rats. We had a rat in here one time and I shot it."

"You *shot* it?"

"Yeah, with a BB pistol. Blam. Dead rat. Here, I'll loan it to you."

I liked the idea of disposing of the rat with a pistol. It was much manlier than traps or poison. Plus, I happen to be a good shot, having grown up with guns. I took Joe's pistol and walked home, trailed by a mutt named Roxy. She didn't belong to Joe and Heather, but she preferred them to her owner, who lived nearby and let Roxy do as she pleased. She was such a character, that dog. She often camped outside my apartment, hoping I'd take her for a ride, and if I drove off without her, she'd chase my car for blocks, panting in my rearview mirror as if to say, "Wait! You forgot *me*!"

Still, she had never come inside my place, not even when I tried to bait her with food, which she'd snatch and eat on my porch. My car was one thing, but my apartment was another. And yet this night, despite my having done nothing to bait her, she followed me inside and jumped on the sofa, where she curled up and slept. I wrote with the pistol next to my computer, waiting for the rat to show itself, but it never did. At one point my friend Chris dropped by with his co-worker Anthony, both startled by a scene that Chris, every so often, still mentions: "Yeah, one time I went over to Duke's place and he was writing with a pistol beside him!"

Roxy peacefully passed the night on my sofa, and I slept after I let her out, and I didn't see the rat when I woke. I never saw it again, in fact. For a while I thought it must have died someplace inside the house after eating poison, but I would've found the corpse if so. To this day I wonder why it left so abruptly.

It must have been frightened by the presence of Roxy, yes? But why did she follow me and spend the night at my house, which, again, was uncharacteristic of her? She must have sensed that something was amiss, and appointed herself my temporary guardian; yet things were often amiss with me — why that night and no other?

Anyway, the rat was gone. And so is Roxy now, and so is Kerry. Roxy was struck and killed by a car the year before Kerry died of cancer: two ghosts in a city that teems with them, and among the many that haunt me.

HOW I BECAME HUMAN

GROWING UP IN a small Southern city, I acquired a racist vocabulary early. This was by no means encouraged by my parents, who were mortified when, at four or so, I loudly referred to a fellow customer at Sears as a nigger. I have no memory of doing that—I was told about it years later—but I'm sure I was baffled by the punishment I received. The kids in my neighborhood used the word "nigger" as a matter of course. To them, it was an appropriate term for a person of color, and I followed suit, even after the Sears incident. Why punish someone for calling a bird a bird? And why would a bird object? So, I think, my reasoning went.

At the time, I barely knew any black people, but that changed when I started school. On my first day of the first grade, a black classmate spoke out of turn and was made to stand in a trash can. I likewise got into trouble for, among other things, spontaneously performing the Tarzan cry, and though I was spared the trash-can treatment, my teacher must have decided I was going to be too much to handle and quickly had me moved to another class. My new teacher, Mrs. Orr, was black, and she told me to have a seat when I arrived one morning in the middle of a lesson. I remained standing and stuck my tongue out at her.

"Why did you do that?" she asked.

I was positive she knew why. Kids and teachers were natural enemies: cats and dogs; cobras and mongooses. That's what I'd learned from TV, but on TV it was funny, and kids who misbehaved were often the most beloved.

So I was shocked when the kids in Mrs. Orr's class didn't laugh or give me looks of complicity when I stuck out my tongue. Instead, they stared blankly: the same response I'd received in my first class when I performed the Tarzan cry.

"Class," said Mrs. Orr, "is this any way to act?"

"Noooooooooooo," said the class in unison, and, cowed, I sat.

Over the few next few days, I continued to annoy, sometimes without trying. For instance, we learned how to write our names, and, being besotted with American Indians, I embellished my name with Indian touches, such as turning the letter *D* into a bow about to shoot an arrow. I thought it demonstrated imagination—a trait my parents prized in me—but Mrs. Orr held up my paper for everyone to see, and said, "Class, is this the way we write our name?"

"Noooooooooooo," said the class in unison. Even at six, I was clearly out of step with my generation.

One overcast day, for some infraction or the other, I was sent into the hall. I was often sent into the hall—a punishment that made no sense to me, since I much preferred the hall to class. I suppose I was meant to reflect on the reason I'd been banished and return contrite, but this time I wasn't invited back. Instead, Mrs. Orr appeared and told me to follow her, and we walked down the hall to another classroom. It must have been recess; the room was empty. Rather than wait in the room for the occupants to return, Mrs. Orr escorted me to a nearby staircase and had me sit on one of the stairs.

"This is going to be your new class," she explained, meaning the empty room. "I think you need a different teacher."

"Is she a nigger, too?" I said.

I said it casually, curious. And Mrs. Orr cried. She cried quietly, and she spoke in a soft voice that pierced my hushed confusion.

"If you learn just one thing from me," she said, "I hope it's that I'm not a nigger."

I don't remember the name of my next teacher. I can't even reconstruct her face, which has merged with the face of my fourth-grade teacher, who was young and white and mean. My first-grade teacher was all of those things, but she eventually warmed to me, and I remember the day I wrote a story about my father killing a water moccasin poised to strike, which so impressed her that she left class to show it to another teacher. (The story was a lie, though we'd been told to write a true account based on personal experience.) I was in her class for the rest of that school year, and Mrs. Orr had me for maybe all of two weeks; but her name is forever engraved in my memory, and so is what she taught me as I sat on the staircase, as if arrested between levels on the scale of evolution.

NO TWO IDENTICAL

SNOW WAS FALLING on my father's farm in Virginia, where I'd returned for the holidays. It had been a while, living in Los Angeles, since I'd seen snow. I went outside for a walk.

It was midafternoon, and the sky was opal colored, the curtain of woods in the distance bluish. I walked down a red-clay road, struck by the quiet and change in acoustics—the faint echoes that followed my footsteps. Every surface was glazed with white, including the backs of silhouetted cattle.

The road crossed a small creek, and the rippling sound caused me to pause. There was a stagnant pool in the creek, created by dead branches, and snowflakes, as they struck the still water, instantly perished, like newborns slain on arrival.

I wept.

II. AMICITIA

ROMANCE, BROMANCE, AND DÉJÀ VU

MY BEST FRIEND in my early L.A. days was a Danish guy I'll call Christoph. I lived on the porch of a house in Silver Lake that I shared with a gay musician, a film student from Austria, yet another film student from Italy, and the birdlike former frontwoman of the noted band A Certain Ratio; and Christoph was a constant guest who'd often stop by at night and drink with me till dawn. Like me, he'd lived in New York, where he played at being a painter, and when I met him, through my Austrian housemate, he was launching his career as a production designer. He eventually progressed to designing blockbusters, and when he returned from far-flung locations, he was always full of gossip. I heard much that I won't repeat, though I'll share this much: if Christoph is to be believed—and, whatever his faults, I can vouch for his credibility—Julia Roberts is a major bitch.

At the beginning, we were as close as brothers. Some even said we looked alike, which, though it wasn't true, pleased me considerably, since Christoph was adored by women. But that soon led to a problem. He became involved with the Italian film student, whom I liked also, and when the news broke, I was estranged from Christoph for months.

Then he became involved with another Italian girl, who was related to the first. I was crazy about that girl. I'd marked her for myself. But one night a mutual friend showed up after seeing her with Christoph, and I threw a fit and alerted her cousin – Christoph's ex – who more or less had her deported. Christoph flew to Europe, where they married, and I didn't speak to either of them for over two years.

During that time I struggled to finish a novel, later abandoned, and spent a few weeks in Livingston, Montana, for research purposes. I was a fixture at a bar famously patronized by Sam Peckinpah, and one night I shot pool there with a guy who reminded me of Christoph. He had a similar smile and the charm it suggested, though he seemed genuinely warm, unlike Christoph, whose smile belied a mosquito-sized heart. I mention the guy in Livingston because he surely influenced the dream of Christoph I had that night. In the dream, Christoph was friendly and contrite, and I woke in a state of forgiveness. Interestingly, since breaking contact with him, I'd never run into Christoph, despite our social overlap, but almost as soon as I got back to L.A., I saw him at a party and we patched things up. He'd divorced the Italian girl for visa reasons, though she still regarded herself as his wife, and I became something of a third wheel, with growing frustration.

One night, when Christoph was out of town, I had drinks with his wife at a dive not far from her house. Every guy who saw this girl was instantly smitten, and after she left, I was asked about her. As I spoke, recounting our history, I drunkenly teared up; and I drove straight to her house and fell to my knees when she opened the door and, clutching her with my head pressed against her belly, told her I loved her. I said it again, shaking her, as if that would help to drive the words deeper.

"I love you," I said.

I could feel her gasp, and, thinking I'd scared her, I stood and apologized.

"Don't be sorry," she said.

She told me she loved me, too. She acknowledged having a strange feeling that we were destined to end up together, which of course was my feeling exactly. It was all very dramatic. She said she was going to faint, and I guided her to a nearby divan, where I sat opposite. We stared at each other in shock. What now? Was she going to leave Christoph?

She wasn't, she announced the next day, after spending the night in reflection. She loved me, she reconfirmed, but she was committed to Christoph, or she was for the time being, since she'd caused such a scandal in her family by eloping with him. I told her I'd wait, and we later fooled around, and I wrote her love letters – beautiful in memory – that she never answered. To my horror, she embarked on an affair with someone else – an actor who later became a TV star – and I cut her out of my life. Yet, astonishingly, I continued to see Christoph, who was aware that I had feelings for her, though, not realizing how far I'd taken them, he dismissed me as a serious rival. The actor, on the other hand, troubled him greatly, as he also obviously troubled me, and Christoph and I would meet and commiserate when his wife went missing.

"She's probably fucking him right now," one of us would say.

"She probably is. That whore."

"I hate her, except I also love her."

"I know just what you mean."

She and Christoph went their separate ways, and she instantly took up with another man, having been spurned by the actor.

After all that and everything that had come before, it seemed my friendship with Christoph was permanent. But that wasn't the case, and the *coup de grace* wasn't a woman but, in the not-so-great Hollywood tradition, a screenplay. Christoph was talking about directing a movie, and I proposed an idea for one, which, while I was away in Belgrade, he fleshed out in a screenplay with a collaborator, denying me credit. I didn't care about the credit. It was the theft of the idea that bothered me, but Christoph wanted to make things even by paying me a nominal sum for a rewrite. I took the money, badly needing it, and improved the script, though Christoph continued to deny me credit. It all came to a head at a barbecue at his house, where he repeatedly irked me by referring to *his* screenplay. Finally I said, "Well, you know, Christoph, it's really *our* screenplay. It was my idea, and I did a rewrite."

Christoph loved power games, and one of his favorites was airing secrets at the worst possible moment, smirking as his victim squirmed. Now I played the same game, foolishly thinking he'd appreciate my cheek. He didn't. A few minutes later I walked into the kitchen, where he was lying in wait. How *dare* I embarrass him in front of his guests! And so *what* if it was my idea? It wasn't that great an idea to start with; it was only because of his input that the script was worth a damn. His face was literally purple. We could easily have come to blows if I'd argued back. But I didn't. I was done with the guy, or I was unless he apologized. He never did, and we haven't spoken or seen each other since.

I don't miss Christoph, but I've been thinking of him lately because I'm now estranged from another friend, who, though it took me a while to recognize it, is very like him. He has a similar charm and winning smile, and he's detached and cocky in ways that bring Christoph to mind. For a period, as with Christoph, we were like brothers, hanging out every day and sometimes drinking till dawn. As with Christoph, he's adored by women, and again as with Christoph, that's led to tension. I once ran into a girl I'd always liked and, learning she was now single, concocted fantasies of romance, only to hear a day later that my friend was seeing her.

But that isn't the reason for our estrangement. It's a complicated situation, long in building, and difficult to resolve due to power games. Neither of us will phone to set things right, though he's occasionally texted invitations to parties or had someone else call to invite me. Either way, he knows there's slim chance of a proper conversation with others around, and there always are, now that he and his new girl are, from what I'm told, John-and-Yoko inseparable. Besides, I expect a more personal touch from friends, and so I don't respond, except—tit for tat—to decline the party invitations with cordial, impersonal texts.

This is not how I typically operate. I'm usually direct to a fault. But that hasn't worked in the past with my friend, so I suppose I'll suffer through this remake of a buddy movie I've seen before and hope for a different ending.

THE ASSHOLES

IT WAS THE Saturday night before Halloween, and a friend's band was playing at a party at a gallery not far from my place in Echo Park. I was in a bad mood, though I don't remember why, since this happened a couple of years ago. Then, too, I'm frequently in a bad mood, which I consider a natural byproduct of being a writer.

Anyway, I drove over to the party and parked a few blocks away, about to head inside when I ran into my buddy Pete on the sidewalk. Pete's one of The Assholes, as this particular group of my friends sometimes refer to themselves. I've always maintained that I'm not *really* an asshole, despite being one of The Assholes, but I can certainly act like an asshole on occasion, and this night was one of them.

Pete was on his way to our friend Wade's car to have a beer. The Assholes always have a cooler of beer on hand. Wade was still inside the gallery, and I sat and drank in his car with Pete. Then Wade and his roommate Bill showed up. It was horrible inside the gallery, they said. It was too hot, too loud, and filled with teenagers dressed in ridiculous costumes. I asked if [unbelievably offensive nickname of disliked acquaintance] was there. Yes, [unbelievably offensive nickname of disliked acquaintance] was there, Wade said, and wearing a ridiculous costume.

"My dad would be so proud of me," he continued. "I'm having a beer with the guys instead of hanging out at some party where everybody looks like a [unbelievably offensive slur]." Pete, who's a regular lady-killer, was getting constant calls and texts from a prospective girlfriend who wanted him to meet her at another party in Hollywood.

"She's a [yet another unbelievably offensive slur]," he told me. "Have you ever had sex with a [unbelievably offensive slur repeated]?"

"Yeah, but she was only partly a [same unbelievably offensive slur]."

"That doesn't count."

He wanted to go to the second party, but Wade wanted to go home. Pete ran back to the gallery to say good night to friends. While he was gone, Wade took off, leaving Bill with me. Pete returned to say that the second party was in the Hollywood Hills behind the Sunset Strip.

"Oh, man," I said. "I don't want to go there. It's Saturday night before Halloween! The traffic's going to be murder!"

"It's going to be great," Pete said. "Come on, let's go. I'm going to make out with a [different unbelievably offensive slur] and you guys can [unbelievably offensive compound verb] her while I'm doing it."

He and Bill got in my car, and I started it and turned down a nearby street, thinking I was taking a shortcut, only to find that the street was blocked with construction equipment and signs that pretty much said not to drive there.

"Keep driving," Bill instructed from the backseat.

There was practically no room to squeeze through, but somehow I did, upending a few of the signs in the process. A couple was walking toward us, the girl in a weird-ass costume, and she appeared to panic when she saw my car, pulling closer to her boyfriend and staring at us with freaked-out eyes as we zoomed past.

"What a [new unbelievably offensive slur]!" said Pete.

"That [still another unbelievably offensive slur]!" concurred Bill.

I couldn't help it; all this anger, at everyone and everything for no good reason, had me in stitches. It always does when I'm hanging with The Assholes. Pete's prospective girlfriend continued to call from the Hollywood party to ask where he was. She gave him directions. Then, when we found the party street, which was very narrow, there was a traffic jam, with some people trying to back up and others trying to drive forward, nobody moving till someone moved first. We were stuck in the middle of this mess, and a woman in the car in front of us beeped her horn and waved her arms frantically as if to say, "You're blocking me!"

"You're blocking *me*!" I yelled; Pete adding, "You [unbelievably offensive slur]!"

It was only because of my deft driving that the traffic jam untangled. We parked and walked up the hill to the party. There were security guards at the door, and we weren't officially invited, but we easily talked our way inside. The two-storey house was packed with affluent assholes in costumes: maids, cops, pirates, astronauts. A DJ was spinning in the living room, and we walked downstairs to the pool behind the house and hung out there for a while. Almost immediately, Pete ran into some asshole he knew, and as they stood there talking, Bill kept whispering something to me. I couldn't make out what he was saying. Finally I realized it was about Pete's asshole friend; that Bill was asking if he should push him into the pool, since he was standing right beside it. I wanted to say yes, but I shook my head no. Then we went upstairs, where Pete found his prospective girlfriend in the kitchen. She was on drugs, it turned out—Bill thought it was ecstasy, but she didn't look like she was on ecstasy to me. She and Pete started talking, and I figured they wanted to be alone, so I walked outside to the balcony. Bill came with me. As we stood there, staring down at the pool, Bill picked up a golf club, which was inexplicably lying on the balcony, and he dared me to throw it over the railing and into the pool.

I did. We watched as it hit the pool with a slight splash, floating there. Nobody by the pool seemed to notice. There was another golf club that Bill suggested I throw also. I did. Again, nobody seemed to notice. Now I got more ambitious, seeing a huge, lit-up jack-o'-lantern on a nearby table.

"Let's throw *that*," I said.

Bill loved that idea. I picked up the jack-o'-lantern and hurled it over the railing. I didn't see it go in, but I heard it. Everybody did. There was a loud splash, followed by screams, which came, I assumed, from people who'd been standing by the pool and were, if not exactly drenched, then a little more wet than they'd been previously. Bill and I quickly exited the balcony.

Pete was still in the kitchen, talking to the girl on drugs.

"Hey, Iron," he said, referring to me by one of my many nicknames. "I'm hungry. Is there anything to eat?"

Bill and I raided the refrigerator. There wasn't much on hand.

"Who owns this place?" I asked Pete.

"Oh, some [unbelievably offensive slur]."

Eventually Bill and I managed to find some frozen chili, a jar of dip, a bag of pretzels, and a couple of frozen veggie burgers. Bill put the veggie burgers in the toaster oven, and I heated up the frozen chili in the microwave, but Pete, whose diet is determined entirely by mood, refused it all. Bill and I ate the veggie burgers, as well as the pretzels. We both declined the chili. We were bored out of our minds.

"Man," Bill said, "I am going to remember that jack-o'-lantern hitting that pool for the rest of my life. That was priceless."

He suggested that we search the premises for more pumpkins. We found a bunch outside. They weren't carved like the first ones. The security guards were lingering nearby, so it took a while before we could move the first of the pumpkins back to the balcony, but another asshole took it away from me as soon as I got there and threw it himself, missing the pool by a good twenty feet. Then Bill and I went for another pumpkin, but just as we got back to the balcony, we were approached by still another asshole who seemed to know the house's owner, as well as what we were planning to do. It was okay if we threw the pumpkin, he said, but don't throw it in the pool, and *especially* don't throw it on the deck.

"Then what's the fucking point of throwing it?" I wanted to ask but didn't. Then a female asshole, costumed like nothing I recognized, took the pumpkin away and threw it herself. It was another bad throw: no loud splash, and no screams afterward. Pete walked up alone and said he wanted to leave.

"Wait," I said. I ran out and smuggled the last pumpkin inside.

"Do you want to make a *really* big mess?" I asked Bill.

"Yes!" he said, with a look of childlike glee.

I threw the pumpkin directly onto the deck. Pulp and seeds sprayed everywhere. We could now leave in triumph. We walked back down the hill, where Pete noticed a couple of girls sleeping in a car. He tapped on the window, trying to wake them, saying, "Want to hang out?" They didn't, understandably. I dropped Bill off, and Pete decided he was hungry; again, he'd declined to eat earlier. He directed me to a Del Taco not far from his apartment. There were too many cars lined up at the drive-thru, so we went inside, but it was crowded there as well. A middle-aged woman dressed like a chicken was standing behind us in line. Other patrons were similarly attired in ridiculous costumes.

"I dare you to say [the most offensive word known to mankind] when you place the order," Pete said to me.

Well, I can never refuse a dare. I got to the front of the line and turned to Pete.

"What do you want to eat, [the most offensive word known to mankind]?" I said to him, loud enough for the guy behind the counter to hear.

"I'll take a macho taco and a [the most offensive word known to mankind] burrito," he said, inserting the word so skillfully that I wasn't sure if the guy behind the counter had heard him.

"Is that all?" he said, straight-faced, not missing a beat.

"Yeah. And throw in some [the most offensive word known to mankind] sauce."

I was sure he'd understood that time. He gave us a look as if to say, "What a couple of assholes."

"He's probably going to spit in our food," I said to Pete.

"No, he's not the one preparing it. But he probably would if he were."

"You worked it in perfectly."

"I've done it before."

Then I noticed that the woman dressed like a chicken was giving us a scathing look, and with that, I *really* felt like an asshole.

On the other hand, she was an asshole herself. I mean, who the hell dresses like a chicken, on Halloween or any other occasion?

Sadly, these days I don't see much of The Assholes.

THE DOUBLE MEANING OF D.R.

I'D JUST WOKEN when the phone rang. It was my friend Fiona, or so I'll refer to her.

"Duke," she said, immediately after saying hello, "I have to warn you: I've had a couple of vodkas."

"This early in the day? What's the problem?"

I've gotten fairly good at this kind of thing since I've slowly transformed from Duke, oft-depressed and occasionally suicidal writer, to Dr. Duke, the go-to guy if you're as oft-depressed and occasionally suicidal as the doctor himself.

Fiona's problem, as I should have anticipated, was her ex, who'd been threatening to remove their young son from her custody. They'd been trying to work out a divorce settlement, and things had lately taken a turn for the worse. Angry e-mails. Intimidating letters from Fiona's attorney. A scene in Fiona's front yard. All of this evoked the turmoil of my parents' divorce when I was a child. And then I wondered why I'd never married.

Fiona cried. She sobbed, in fact. She apologized for sobbing, and I told her it was okay, as any shrink would. Then I tried to advise her.

"You're antagonizing your ex," I said. "I mean, I know he's a jerk, but that's all the more reason why you shouldn't run straight to your attorney when he sends you a threatening e-mail."

She ultimately decided I was right, more or less. She hung up sounding relatively cheerful, and I asked myself if I would later hear from the friend I'll call Ethan. He'd gone broke in a big way, and for a period I would daily spend hours on the phone with him, mostly listening as he deliberated his options.

"Well," he would say, "if the bank comes to throw me out of my house, I'm going to stand on the porch with a flare gun and shoot it at the sky and scream, 'THEY'RE THROWING ME OUT OF MY HOUSE!' Because I want everyone in this neighborhood to know about it. And maybe then I'll go live in a trailer. Yes, I think I might find a trailer somewhere in the desert, because I don't think I'll be in a position to rent anything in the city, and, besides, I don't want to live next to noisy people blasting awful music. And I honestly don't think I'd mind living in a trailer. I think it would be an adventure, you know? Or maybe I'll just kill myself. I mean, I'll save that as a last option, if I can't even afford a trailer, but I'm not afraid to kill myself, because I've had a good run, you know? I mean, I am certainly not going to spend the last chapter of my life working at a Denny's—if I could even *get* a job at Denny's. I'm not qualified to do *anything*."

At that point, which arose more than once, I reminded Ethan that, like him, I wasn't qualified to do anything, aside in my case from writing; and also, like him, I was broke to the point of desperation.

"Yes, I know you are. Well, I'll tell you what: if I don't kill myself and I do get a trailer, you can come live with me in the desert. I mean, you'll have to pitch a tent in the yard, because we both know it'll never work if you live *in* the trailer. But it wouldn't be so bad to live in a tent, would it? You could write in the tent all day, and then at night you could come inside and we could have dinner, and then you could go sleep in the tent. It would be an adventure, you know?"

He was flippant, yet serious. I told him I'd consider it. Any shrink—even a lay shrink—knows that you don't swat down the ideas of desperate people, which would only make them feel worse. Besides, Ethan has often acted as my shrink when I've called at the hour of the wolf.

Sometimes, even a casual call can lead to an intake session. I recently phoned an acquaintance to invite her to a reading from my novel, and she told me she couldn't attend because she'd just been served with divorce papers.

"He's been living part-time in Texas," she volunteered about her husband (whom I'd never met), "and he's been having an affair, and I think he's had a private detective spying on me so he can get a better deal in court. And he put out a restraining order on me! I've never done a *thing* to him! Not one *thing*! And we have a *child*! Oh my God, how am I going to support my *child*?"

This went on for at least an hour, which I'd say is about average for an intake session. I offered to put Fiona in touch with her, figuring the two would have much to discuss. Unfortunately, I didn't know anybody to whom I could refer the woman I'll call Amy, who's the wife of a friend from my New York days. They moved to L.A. not long after I did, and had two daughters, and Amy was wearing herself out with worry about them. She'd enrolled them in a private school that she and her husband couldn't afford, but she insisted, since, among other reasons, the school has a dress code that doesn't allow for Hannah Montana T-shirts and the like, which Amy is afraid her daughters will covet. She doesn't even let her daughters watch television, she's so concerned they'll start pining for this ridiculous thing or that one. A highbrow artist who's more than earned her many accolades, Amy loathes pop culture. I sympathize. I love underground pop culture, but I generally dislike the TV kind.

Amy's anxiety increasingly overtook her. She tried a number of psychotropic drugs, none of which did the trick. Eventually, she called while I was browsing one night at Amoeba Music to say she was in the hospital.

"I'm having electroshock therapy," she announced in the calmest voice I'd ever heard, at least from her. "I know what you're thinking; it's bad, but electroshock therapy has come a long ways. I can't even tell you how much better I feel."

How and when did I become Dr. Duke? Maybe it started fifteen years ago, when a friend rang me up to threaten suicide because his fiancée had called off their engagement to go work on an ostrich farm. He was certain she was diddling somebody else, and, sure enough, she soon married a fellow ostrich farmer. Still, I managed to talk my friend down, and he's now married to someone who would never contemplate going to work on an ostrich farm.

I suppose I give good advice. It never seems as though I give good advice, since it never seems to get followed, though I've occasionally had people tell me that they left such-and-such job or moved to such-and-such city because of something I said, in some cases years before. I just wish I could give good advice to myself. Therapy, for me, was a bust. The only half-effective therapist I had since high school turned out to be an aspiring novelist—a novelist who, by his own proud admission, never read novels—and our sessions concluded shortly after he asked me to read his manuscript and I failed to sufficiently praise it. Meantime, I was once so low that, at four in the morning, I called the suicide hotline to pull me back from the brink. A surly male voice answered. I froze.

"Hello?" repeated the surly voice.

I was about to say something when the line went dead with a decisive click.

I'd been hung up on. By the suicide hotline. Even I, a novice, would never do something like that.

CUTTY SARKED

TWO AND A half years ago my friend Brin Friesen was visiting L.A. from Vancouver and I arranged for him to read from his recently published novel, *Sic*, at a place called the Tribal Café on a stretch in Filipinotown known for crack dealing. I organized a whole night, in which I would read from my own novel, *Banned for Life*, and afterward I'd screen a film directed by another friend who regularly, and kindly, supplied me with writing jobs.

I'm always nervous before readings, so I brought along a bottle of Bushmills, which I shared with the audience. It went quickly, so I asked my mentor, George, if he'd mind grabbing another bottle from a store across the street. (I met George when I was a teenager living in New York, and it's due in no small part to him that I became a writer; he was the first bona-fide intellectual I knew, and one of the few intellectuals I know still.) He fatefully returned with a liter bottle of Cutty Sark.

I did a number of shots during Brin's reading. Then I drank several bottles of water to dissipate the buzz. Got to clear my head for my own reading, yes? I consider myself a modest type, but I have to say, I was in excellent form that night. It didn't feel like a reading at all; it felt like a punk-rock show, with my friend Pete throwing beer cans, and me yelling at somebody else for ordering a cappuccino and so causing the fucking machine to grind. In fact, *Banned for Life* is about punk rock, and a lot of my friends are musicians, and several came up after the reading to say how much they enjoyed it. For once I didn't doubt them. Then the movie started, and I figured I deserved a drink.

And drink I did. I sat at a table with that huge bottle of Cutty Sark; and I'd barely eaten all day; and I'd barely slept after staying up late to clean my apartment, since my eviction-minded landlords were coming by to inspect it – this after, a day before, I returned from San Francisco, where I also failed to get much sleep, between the barhopping and the snores at the hostel and the sheer excitement of being out of L.A. I mean, who can sleep after a jailbreak?

So I was clearly in no shape to be drinking so much (as if *any* shape were ideal), but did that stop me? No, it did not. I kept knocking back shot after shot, with no sense of how much I was downing, meantime braying at the movie.

Then, next thing I knew, I was standing outside on the curb and a car was pulling up, and people were telling me to get in the car. I had no idea how I'd gotten from the café to the curb, just as I had no idea what I meant when I heard myself say that I'd fucked up the whole night and nobody was ever going to speak to me again. I didn't realize I was coming out of a blackout. But, as directed, I got into the car, where George was behind the wheel, and he dropped me off at my place. Then my friend Bryce showed up, which was odd, considering the hour. I could tell he was concerned about me, but I was clueless as to why. I knew I was drunk, of course, but I didn't know just how drunk I was, being so drunk.

Well, Bryce stayed for maybe forty-five minutes, and we talked (with some difficulty on my part), mostly about the reading. He was full of compliments, which meant a great deal, since his band, Die Princess Die, was and is an all-time favorite. Then he left, and I was about to get some much-needed sleep when I realized my car was parked on the street beside the café, and I would likely get a ticket when 7 A.M. rolled around, or, worse, my car could be towed. I wasn't about to let that happen, so I walked – that is, staggered – all the way back to Filipinotown and drove home. By then it was daylight, and I realized I was missing a camera I'd brought to the reading, so I called George and said, "Hey, do you know what happened to my camera?" I had it with me in his car, he said, and I suddenly spied it, right by the phone. Then he shared a few details about the previous night.

First of all, he said, I tripped outside the café and knocked over a row of sandwich boards, one after the other, and fell on top of them, like a stunt in a slapstick comedy circa 1920. Afterward, he said, I screamed things at my friends like "Who *are* you people? I don't need you!" He couldn't believe I had no memory of this, which I didn't and don't. I'd never had a blackout before (and I've never had one since).

I called other friends, who provided more details. It seemed I'd fallen out of my chair during the movie – repeatedly – and broken the bottle of Cutty Sark and kicked the shards across the room. I not only fell on top of the sandwich boards but collapsed in the street, where one person said I "rolled around" while shouting things like "I am *so* punk rock!" and "Punk rock for all!" Then, after being restrained, I sat on the curb and said, "I live by the code; fuck everybody," over and over again. Even I was stumped as to what "code" I had in mind.

It gets better. I screamed, "I will never write for you again!" at my director friend. I tried to choke Pete, who's likewise in Die Princess Die, and who, I was told, was pissed. Not, I'm sure, that I tried to choke Pete in earnest, even though he had been throwing beer cans at me during the reading.

I called George again and said, "Jesus Christ, you didn't even tell me the worst of it! I must really look like an asshole!"

"I don't think so. I think your friends kind of see you as Keith Richards."

"Well, I'm *not* Keith Richards. And if I'm going to get drunk and shout shit, why couldn't it be cool? I mean, why couldn't I say, 'I'm the Lizard King; I can do anything!' instead of 'I am *so* punk rock!' *Man*, is that lame. You think I should call everybody and apologize?"

"You think Keith Richards should apologize for doing heroin?"

You're a pal, George.

I slept, and later that day, stiff gaited and cotton brained, I saw that I'd parked my car in the middle of the street. It made me think of the O.J. Simpson case, when the cops went to O.J.'s house to tell him his ex had been murdered and they noticed that his car was parked kind of funny, which led to his becoming a suspect. But his car was parked sanely compared to mine. If one of my exes had been murdered the night of my reading and the cops had seen where I'd left my car, I'd be dead now. They would've pulled their guns and said, "Freeze, killer!" and if I'd have so much as flinched, they would've opened fire, turning me into a 6'2" salt shaker.

I called Pete and the director to mend fences. I saw my friend Hawke, who told me that he'd kept a fragment of the broken Cutty Sark bottle as a memento. He'd brought a friend to the reading, someone who'd been torn as to how to spend his night: go to a punk show or go to my reading.

"I told him this was going to be a punk reading," Hawke said. "He asked what I meant. Well, he sure knows now!"

WHAT CHILD IS THIS?

A RELATIVE IS apparently angry at me, or so I was told by another relative. Fortunately, it has nothing to do with my contributions to The Nervous Breakdown (though this piece may well compound the situation). Rather, in his (erroneous) view, I slighted still another relative, so, on that relative's unrequested behalf, I'm being given the silent treatment.

Meantime, last week, while in the middle of extremely trying financial circumstances (including the death of my car), a friend texted to ask why I'd been "talking shit" about him. I could only guess as to his meaning. I'd recently discussed him with a mutual acquaintance, specifically regarding what I considered a pattern of rudeness. I should've spoken to my friend, as opposed to *about* him, but I did so because I didn't want to make a big deal out of it. However, our acquaintance seems to have decided a big deal was in order, and tattled.

André Malraux – the French statesman and author of, among other books, *Man's Hope* – once asked a priest what he'd learned over the years, and the priest replied that there was no such thing as a grown-up. I'm rapidly coming to the same conclusion. I've been astonished, throughout my adult life, at how childish people can be. Not that I exclude myself. I'm, alas, thin-skinned and so can be quick to take umbrage, though I'm always prepared to admit I'm wrong, as I frequently am.

But giving people the silent treatment is something I haven't done for years, just as I've gotten far better at keeping the secrets of others. I used to be bad about that. Once, when I was living in New York, I introduced one gay friend to another, and they promptly began a romance. Then my friend John, who likewise knew them both, told me one of them was cheating with a musician – and I use that term loosely, seeing that the only song he could play was the theme from *Valley of the Dolls*, or so I gathered when I attended one of his shows, during which he played the theme from *Valley of the Dolls* repeatedly, with only minor variations, on a synthesizer. Anyway, he was cheating with my friend, and his boyfriend knew this unbelievably hot English girl (she strongly resembled the 1970s horror-movie actress Anulka Dziubinska), and I was fairly certain she liked me, because maybe an hour after we met, she started kicking me. (Aggression is almost always a good sign.) But I wanted to be sure, so I pumped my friend for information, which he agreed to supply on the condition that I tell him anything I knew about his boyfriend, whom he suspected of cheating. Well, I figured he should know. I mean, he already suspected anyway, and I just had to learn if that English girl liked me. So I told him, without naming John, my source. Then, literally a day later, I was standing with John at the corner of Avenue A and East 4th Street when the *Valley of the Dolls* guy rolled up on a bicycle and said, "John, did you tell [the aggrieved] that I've been seeing [the cheater]? It must have been you, because you and your ex-girlfriend are the only ones who know." John, of course, denied it, and the *Valley of the Dolls* guy raced off on his bike like Almira Gulch in *The Wizard of Oz* to confront John's ex. He might even have tortured her, which he could easily have accomplished by turning on his synthesizer. By then I'd confessed my loose lips to John, who was cool about it, though he got quite a tongue lashing from his ex, and I looked like the ass I was.

Still, I learned something: never betray a confidence. Which is not to say that I didn't do it again—even the most important lessons require reinforcement. But I have gotten much better about it, and I try hard not to sulk or self-dramatize or break things when they aren't working to my satisfaction (especially phones, computers, and DVD players), which are all childish characteristics I'm afraid I continue to demonstrate on occasion. And I try to be a good guy, yet every day seems to bring the potential for a new misunderstanding and, with it, the possible termination of a relationship that previously seemed solid.

In fact, I live with the dread of losing friends. Sometimes people grow apart—that I understand—but I've been through so many dime-poker squabbles and lost friends because of them.

On the other hand, I sometimes wonder if friends even exist; if maybe what we call friends are people who bond because of temporary necessity, and once the necessity has passed, the friendship follows.

Of course, this is a terrible way of looking at things, but, hey, I'm going through a tough time at the moment. Also, I think I may have been traumatized in the matter of friendship by Jay, who was my best friend from ages nine through nineteen. One day I'll have to write about our crime sprees, but those came after the critical period in the fifth grade, when he decided he had *another* best friend, this redneck named Blaine. I couldn't understand what he saw in Blaine, who looked like a ventriloquist's puppet and later took to wandering the streets alone with a boombox blasting country music—*bad* country music. But he and Jay started hanging out, and Jay would make it clear to me that he didn't want me around at those times; and once, when it was the three of us together, Jay suddenly said, "One, two, three, go!" and he and Blaine took off running by prearranged agreement and disappeared. I waited, but they didn't come back. Then I went home and cried, and to make matters worse, Jay and Blaine were lurking outside, and the next day at school Jay came up and said, "You didn't have to cry about it."

Another time, when we were supposed to go to his house and play records and watch movies (we were both music and movie nuts), he decided he wanted to go over to Billy Pollack's house instead. I said, "Oh, man, there's nothing to do at Billy Pollack's house. He's boring." But, because I wanted to hang out with Jay, I went with him to Billy Pollack's house, where I, in fact, had a great time playing kickball, and as Jay and I were about to leave, I saw him whisper something to Billy Pollack, who walked up and said, "So I'm boring, huh?" and I got in a fight with him.

Yes, maybe my dark view of friendship, which usually isn't dark, goes back to Jay. But getting the silent treatment and having grown men tell tales out of school doesn't much lighten my view of humanity. And now I've probably pissed off somebody else by publishing this puerile mess. Hell, there are microbes in the air that, having found their groove, no doubt hate me every time I move.

Fucking babies.

THAT'S WHAT I'VE BEEN TRYING TO TELL YOU

WE MET IN New York when I read for a part in a play she'd written. She didn't cast me. I struck her as being too intelligent for the part, or so she told me later by way of softening the blow. She'd done some acting herself, mostly in musical theater, where she excelled as a dancer. Then she hurt her back, and so turned to playwriting, graduating from the Yale School of Drama—an impressive achievement for a girl from a small town in Arkansas.

She was pretty, though she didn't believe she was. She had a dancer's lithe build, dark hair, and fair features that came off as wan in photos. She walked daintily, with mincing steps, and her voice had a kind of tremor, hinting at something brittle at her core. Still, she definitely attracted attention on the street, which surprised and, at times, amused her.

We didn't get involved right away. She was with somebody else when we met, and we gradually began an affair that ended before I left New York for L.A. Then, with a new boyfriend, she also moved to L.A., where she, like me, wrote screenplays. Two of her scripts were produced, one with a lot of fanfare, though we seldom saw each other during that period, her boyfriend being jealous of me. Eventually, when they were done, she and I resumed.

She influenced my writing considerably, not so much in style as the fact of her encouragement. She was the first serious writer I knew, so praise from her went a long way. But she was finally competitive as a writer, and grew stingy with praise over time. I would show her a script or story I'd written, and she'd say things like: "Well, I suppose it's pretty good…for its genre."

We fought about that. We also fought when I dared to criticize her fellow Arkansan Bill Clinton. We fought about almost everything, including clumsy remarks on my part. Once, when we were discussing our aborted affair in New York, I said, "I think I was afraid you weren't cool enough" – meaning I was a rocker type, while she still listened to show tunes. She never let me live it down. Every time we fought afterward, she'd say at some point: "Well, as you know, I'm not *cool*."

We broke up and got back together again. We did this several times before we decided we were better off as friends, but even then we fought. She wasn't a heavy drinker, but when she did drink, I knew we were likely to fight. She'd phone to needle me, often late at night, and I'd say, "Have you been drinking?"

"Why?"

"You're trying to pick a fight."

"Yeah, well. That's what people who aren't *cool* do."

In spite of myself, I almost always took the bait, and she almost always hung up on me. Nothing riled me more, as she knew, and one night after she did it still again, I called her back and left a message when she naturally didn't answer.

"Don't you ever call me again!" I said. "And I mean *ever*! I don't want to ever hear from you again! We're fucking done!"

I don't remember what prompted that fight, though I know, and knew, she was going through a difficult time. Her screenwriting career had fallen apart, and she was working a Christmas job in retail. She didn't know where, or if, she'd find a job after the first of the year. She sometimes spoke of returning to Arkansas.

So things stood when we stopped talking. It was a period when I fell out with a number of people, but she was the only one I missed. Was she okay? Was she working? Did she go back to Arkansas? Yet I couldn't bring myself to contact her, just as, for a year and a half, she didn't contact me.

Then she sent me a letter. I recognized her handwriting the second I saw the envelope, and I noted the return address in Arkansas. I was sure the contents would amount to an analysis of our relationship. She'd sent me such letters in the past.

But this letter was different. She described a pain in her chest that came on while she was still in California. The doctors initially blamed the pain on acid reflux. Eventually, when the pain intensified, an MRI was performed, revealing a large tumor in her lung. The tumor was too close to her heart to be removed. She was diagnosed with Stage IV lung cancer, and was now undergoing chemotherapy in Little Rock, where she was living with her sister.

I was floored, of course. She'd always been a hypochondriac—a frequent cause of fights—but even hypochondriacs get sick. Still, lung cancer? Yes, she smoked, but not much: a cigarette a day, if that.

I called immediately. She answered with a hoarse voice. She was weak from the chemo, she said, but she'd gotten the results of her latest tests, which were promising: the tumor was shrinking. Still, she emphasized, the prognosis for lung cancer is never good: at best, she might live for another five years. She attributed the cancer to depression, not smoking.

We talked about the fight that led to our long estrangement—what was that about, anyway? We laughed when neither of us could remember. Despite her illness, she sounded good—that is, clearheaded. We got on better than we had in years. At least, I thought, the cancer had accomplished that much.

She asked me to come see her. I would, I promised, but she was officially in remission the next time we spoke, and there seemed to be no special hurry. I told her I would send her the novel I'd recently finished. In fact, it wasn't finished, but I thought otherwise. I didn't expect her to read it; I simply wanted her to see the manuscript and realize that, like me, she could write a novel. Maybe if she started one, it would help her to further rally.

She read my novel. She liked it, she said in an offhand way, as if she didn't like it at all. I was irked. She was as competitive as ever, I thought. The cancer had changed nothing. We often spoke on the phone during her summer of remission, with touches of our old tension, though we never openly fought as we'd done in the past.

Then new test results came back. The cancer had spread: it was now in her ovaries as well as her brain. The tumors in her brain were tiny, but if they grew, they could result in dementia or seizures or both. She was more frightened by brain cancer than she was of death, she told me.

The doctors thought she was a poor candidate for another round of chemo, since she'd been so weakened by the first round. Still, the choice was hers: she could take a chance on the chemo, but her quality of life, even if the chemo extended her life, might be poor, to say the least.

She ultimately decided against the chemo. She did, however, have radiation for the brain cancer. It worked: the tumors disappeared.

One night in November we had an especially long talk on the phone. Her final wish had been to see Paris again, she said, but she was now too sick for such a big trip. Instead, she wanted to spend a weekend in San Francisco, where she could see the ocean one last time. She could also see the ocean in L.A., of course, but she didn't want to return to L.A. She asked if I'd meet her in San Francisco. Absolutely, I said; how soon did she have in mind?

"Well, that's what I've been trying to tell you," she said. "I won't last until the spring."

I'm still struck by her phrasing. Somehow, despite the constant updates about her condition, I'd failed to understand that time was running out. Now I understood. She said she had to go. I couldn't speak, knowing that I'd cry if I did.

"Are you there?" she asked. I made a small noise to let her know I was.

"It's okay," she said. "It's all going to be okay."

"It's *not* going to be okay," I barely managed, my voice cracking.

"Yes, it is. It's okay. It's all going to be okay."

I was overcome with depression. It wasn't just her. My novel, I now recognized, needed a lot of work, and I was unable to do the work, since I kept having to write screenplays for practically nothing. It was Christmas, and I hadn't seen my family in a few years, so it was either let another year pass without seeing them or use my rent money to pay for a flight home. My landlords would try to evict me. My novel would never be finished. I wished I were dead, and said as much the next time she called. I knew it was an awful thing to say to someone on the verge of death, but it was nonetheless true, and I wanted to be able to speak to her as I used to do, without pretense. Maybe she would appreciate my honesty, I thought, especially since everyone she knew was bound to be tiptoeing around her. Surely those people were depressed at times, but they would never admit it—not to her. Here was a chance to be herself—a person who'd struggled with depression, like me—instead of, generically, a person who was dying.

But she was understandably aghast that I would say such a thing. I tried to explain my reasoning, selfish as it was, but she wasn't interested in listening. She made an excuse to get off the phone and quickly hung up, and I flew home for Christmas feeling worse than ever. When I returned, I saw that she'd sent me a card. The front of the card was white, except for a few words in black:

DANCE

as if no one is watching

SING

as if no one is listening

LIVE

as if each day were your last

Inside, she'd written to chide me for what I'd said on the phone. She was "weary" of my "inability to accept change," she wrote. That was an old complaint. She'd always seen me as clinging to youth, and it was true, I did cling, but she, unlike me, had never been invested in youth culture.

Yes, the cancer had changed nothing. Our new relationship – the one that started with the letter that broke our long silence – had followed our old relationship: we'd gotten along wonderfully, followed by tension and a fight of a kind. And yet, she wrote in the card, she forgave me, which felt like final words.

I called her again and again. She didn't answer. I wondered if her condition had deteriorated or if she was simply avoiding me. Then one night the phone rang, and by the time I got to the phone, the call had gone to voice mail. I listened to the message. It was her. She was in the hospital, she said, where the doctors were trying to resolve some problems, including fluid in her lungs, and she expected to go home in a couple of days. She could barely speak, her voice was so hoarse, and I decided not to call back right away. Let her rest, I thought. I would call in a few days, after she'd gone home. For now, it was gratifying simply to know she was alive.

Weeks passed. She didn't respond to my messages. I Googled for an obituary and found nothing.

One night a friend called to ask if I'd heard from her. I hadn't, I told him, and hung up and Googled again. An obituary came up this time. She'd died a few days after she called from the hospital. Why didn't I call back right away?

I was too staggered to cry. Her tremulous voice, her dainty walk, her lithe body, which I knew so well: how could it be here, then gone forever? I couldn't quite wrap my head around it, despite the months I'd had to prepare.

But I did cry later, and never when I thought I would. For instance, seven months after she died, I went to San Francisco to see friends, and I thought of her as I crossed the Oakland Bridge. I didn't cry then; I cried when I spoke of her to my friends in a North Beach bar, and they'd never met her. She and I had talked about getting together in San Francisco, I blubbered, and here I was without her. I could tell my friends didn't understand. I didn't understand myself. I'd known a lot of people who'd died, but she was different, and so was the way I grieved.

One day my friends and I took a bus to the beach at the foot of the Golden Gate Bridge. A tickling breeze was blowing off the bay, and gentle waves were breaking, and I remembered her wish to see the ocean one last time. Why the ocean? Maybe, I thought, to be reminded of her smallness in the scheme of things, as we're all small, except to those whose lives we've changed.

I walked to a shelf of rocks, where, hidden from my friends, I leaned down and tried to write her name with my finger in the sand beside the water. I did this repeatedly, never able to finish before a wave swept up and erased the letters. Finally I managed to write a whole phrase, which remained for only a moment.

The phrase included her name, preceded by the three words that I never sufficiently expressed but always deeply felt, even when we weren't speaking at a time when speaking was still possible.

(Top) Already, around the time I started school, problematic, as per the whispered suggestions of the stuffed snake around my neck. *(Bottom)* Awaiting exploitation by a child pornographer. I wouldn't have to wait for long.

(Top) Grand View, the only home I've ever recognized as such. The truncated left wing of the house was rebuilt after being demolished by cannonfire during the Civil War. *(Bottom left)* The mistress of Grand View, my angelic grandmother Cornelia, smiling despite the demonic grandson she holds. *(Bottom right)* The tow-headed demon, a year or two older, atop a toy tractor on the Grand View lawn.

(Above) Reading *The Richmond Times-Dispatch* at Grand View during a weekend visit from New York. *(Left)* Embarking on a hunting trip during another weekend visit from New York, after I've discovered punk.

GEORGE PORCARI

GEORGE PORCARI

(Top) Posing as Macbeth, with my then-girlfriend posing as Lady Macbeth, for an art-school project assigned to my New York roommate George. *(Bottom)* On the roof of the apartment building where George and I lived on the Lower East Side.

GEORGE PORCARI

AUTHOR'S COLLECTION

(Top) An embarrassing memento from the Lower East Side: emaciated and squalid me, asleep on the floor. *(Bottom)* Roxy, the mutt whose very presence could eliminate a rat where human effort failed.

FOLLOW THE LINE

Readings from new and upcoming works

JIM RULAND, BRYAN PRICE, SCOTT O'CONNOR,
DARYL "DUKE" HANEY
WITH MUSIC BY BLACK POWDER

SEPT 27 8:00 AT TRIBAL cafe
1651 W TEMPLE ST LOS ANGELES CA
www.tribalcafe.com /(213)483-4459

(Above left) A flier, featuring the combined faces of Jim Morrison and Arthur Rimbaud, for a reading at the Tribal Café. *(Above right)* My second attempt at killing my friend Pete, after unsuccessfully trying to choke him to death at the Tribal Café. *(Right)* Pete, characteristically holding a beer, with our mutual friend Burke at a Die Princess Die show at the Echo.

(Top) Die Princess Die: Pete, Ely, me (a.k.a. Stu Sutcliffe), Bryce, and Danny, at Ely's wedding in San Diego. *(Bottom)* A typical outcome of a DPD show, minus the blood.

(Top) Shredding my voice at the Knitting Factory in 2005. *(Bottom)* Again shredding my voice on the floor at Three Clubs in 2009. The band, Memory, includes Gregg, who smirks down at me, and Danny and Bryce of Die Princess Die. Phil, the bass player, is off-camera.

III. MUSICA

ICE CREAM, HEROIN, AND A CHANCE ENCOUNTER AT RALPH'S

IN THE SUMMER of 2002, I'd just returned to L.A. from Belgrade, where I could live cheaply and so work full time on *Banned for Life*. To my frustration, the book still required extensive surgery, and one night, in lieu of taking an ax to my computer, I drove to Ralph's Supermarket on Glendale Boulevard. It was three in the morning, but there was a longish line at the cash register, and the customer immediately behind me was Elliott Smith. The checker wandered off, and I wondered if I should say anything to Elliott.

Elliott and I were strangers, but I'd once given his girlfriend – let's call her Kate – a ride home from an …And You Will Know Us by the Trail of Dead show, where she'd been accosted by a deranged groupie type who'd been stalking Elliott. Kate was Scottish; gregarious but fiery – a friend of my friends in Trail of the Dead. At the time, she and Elliott were living in a bungalow complex in Los Feliz. The bungalows looked like Tudor dioramas at a history-themed amusement park. (I would later recognize them as a key location in David Lynch's *Mulholland Drive*.) We sat in my car for close to an hour while Kate cried and talked about Elliott's problems, hinting at his fondness for heroin, which hardly came as a shock, considering the many allusions to heroin in his songs: "The White Lady

Loves You More," "Needle in the Hay," and so on. She thought L.A. was bad for him, and she was trying to get him to move with her to Scotland, where in theory he'd be safe from pernicious influences.

It was a curious exchange – the sudden intimacy of it all – and now, almost a year later, here was Elliott, standing behind me at Ralph's with a carton of ice cream in either hand – in fact, I think he was holding three. Funny that I remember what he was buying when I don't remember what I was buying myself. It couldn't have been liquor – not at that hour.

The checker kept us waiting, and I turned to Elliott and mentioned the ride I'd given Kate. They'd had a fight, he said – that's why he'd gone to the store. To me it explained the ice cream: sweet compensation for a bitter spat. He was obviously troubled, but, then, he was Elliott Smith – what did I expect? At one point he said something about getting into therapy, and I said, "Well, therapy's so pat, you know. I'm not sure it'll work if you happen to be a genius."

"I'm not a genius," he half-laughed, adding that his father was a therapist. One of us – it was probably him – raised the subject of heroin. I told him I used to fool around with heroin, and I liked it, but not enough to form a dependency.

"Oh, I loved it," he said. "Right from the start." I thought, "Jesus Christ, I'm standing here talking about doing heroin with Elliott Smith at Ralph's Supermarket!" The checker returned, and after paying for our various items, Elliott and I walked outside to the parking lot, where I expected him to quickly get into his car and drive away. Instead, we continued talking for another fifteen minutes, mostly about his spiritual malaise. I tried to advise him, but I wasn't at my best, since I still couldn't get over the fact that I was talking to Elliott Smith. Then, after I returned home, I did something that now makes me wince: I posted a message on a music-oriented Yahoo! group to which I belonged to brag about having bumped into Elliott. How about that, people? Ain't I kewl?

I never saw him again, though shortly after that encounter, he broke up with Kate and moved to an apartment a few blocks from mine in Echo Park. That's where he was living when he killed himself with a stab to the heart in October 2003. I thought of Kate when the news broke: her saying that L.A. was bad for him; her wish that they could live together in Scotland. I thought of the way he looked that night at Ralph's – bad skin, witchy features, scraggly hair – yet there was something instantly likeable about him. I read somewhere that he took umbrage at hearing his music described as "fragile," but it *was* fragile, and so was he.

A friend of mine regularly meets with a psychic, and he told me that during one of their sessions, Elliott came through. They'd never met, but my friend is a musician, so they'd traveled common ground. Through the psychic, Elliott said that he only wished he'd known how much his music meant to people while he was alive. Still, he was doing well on the other side. My friend asked about Kurt Cobain. "Kurt's divided," my friend reported Elliott as saying, explaining that in the afterlife souls can sometimes be spread apart.

Unlike my friend, I don't place much stock in the metaphysical, though I try to keep an open mind. I don't pretend to understand the mysteries of life. I have my guesses, but I know that's all they are. Still, I've never quite shaken the notion that I squandered the chance that night to say something that might've kept Elliott from killing himself. Yes, we were strangers, and it was only a brief exchange, but I once saved myself from getting mauled by an attacking pit bull by freezing rather than fleeing – a tactic I'd picked up years before while channel surfing. Sometimes something as random as that can make for a world of difference. And now I'm writing about a talk at Ralph's Supermarket at three in the morning, and that by itself tells me that every moment counts, or it can potentially, if you haven't given up on the world altogether.

DELIVERING PIZZAS, LOSING PHONES, AND STALKING THE WALKMEN: A NIGHT IN HELL

I FUCKING LOVE the Walkmen.

Do you know the Walkmen? If you don't, you should. I've been crazy about that band ever since I first heard "The Rat," their best-known song; and last night—a few hours ago, as I write these words—they played in Los Angeles.

Unfortunately, I couldn't go. I had to work my part-time job as a pizza maker/delivery guy. That's how bad things are at the moment. I've been making my living as a writer for years, and now I've hit a wall. It's probably a temporary wall, but it's still a wall, due entirely to America's economic crisis.

Thanks, all you people who couldn't afford houses but insisted on buying them! Thanks, all you real-estate brokers for setting up deals you knew wouldn't pan out! You guys are the best!

It's not that I mind working a so-called real job; it's just that I'm a bit rusty at that sort of thing, having been out of the real-job world for some time. And of course the pizzeria people put me on the schedule for Wednesday night, when the Walkmen were in town, and I couldn't say no, since it was either that or Thursday night, when I'm doing a reading from my novel. And I'd wanted to give the Walkmen a copy of the novel because I listened to their music constantly during my final year of work on it, and also because I know they're literate guys, even though I don't know them personally. I know they're literate because I've repeatedly read that they've been writing a novel together. All of them. Collectively. Which, in rock & roll terms, makes them *very* literate. It makes them practically lit professors. Almost no rocker types read, let alone attempt to write novels, collectively or not.

Anyway, I go to work at the pizzeria, and something is wrong with my brain. I mean, I keep forgetting *everything*. I rush out the door without the address of the place where I was supposed to deliver, only discovering I'm missing it fifteen minutes later, when the pizzeria calls to say, "Hey, do you know where you're going? You can't, because you left the bill here." I get lost – repeatedly. I end up delivering one guy's pizzas two hours late because I can't find his street, and he's called the pizzeria to complain. I neglect to have someone else sign her credit card thing. I make mistake after mistake, and I just know I'm going to get fired after working only two days. And I surely will; I just haven't heard about it yet.

Meantime, as I'm rushing about lost and forgetting everything, my friend Bryce texts me with: *You working tonight? I'm going over to see the Walkmen and I have a plus-one.* I text him back: *Yes, I'm fucking working.* He texts me again, from the show: *Wow, what a set of pipes.* (This refers to the tremendous voice of the Walkmen frontman, Hamilton Leithauser, which has to be heard live to be fully appreciated.) I text Bryce back: *Fuck off.*

Then, mercifully, my shift ends, and I decide I'm going to go home, get a copy of my book, and drive to the El Rey theater, where the Walkmen are playing, and give them my book, even if I *didn't* get to see the show.

I charge down the freeway. I've almost never driven this fast. I'm driving like Steve McQueen in *Bullitt*. I park about three blocks away and walk up, and there, amazingly, is Bryce, outside the El Rey with two girls.

It's only amazing because Bryce is in front of the El Rey, not because he's with two girls. Bryce is annoyingly handsome.

"Where are the Walkmen?" I ask him.

"They were just here two seconds ago," he says. "They were standing right here."

"Where did they go?"

"I don't know. I mean, literally, two seconds ago, they were all standing here."

I explain my insane scheme to give them a copy of my novel. Then one of the girls says, "Oh, hey, there's the drummer."

"Don't look," I say, immediately before walking over to the drummer, who's getting into somebody's car with cymbals underarm. I tell Bryce and the girls not to look because I'm very embarrassed to be seen doing what I'm about to do. It's so *teenaged*.

But I do it. I walk over to the drummer and say, "Hey, I just wanted to give you this," and I explain why. "I was listening to you guys like a motherfucker while I was working on it," I say. "You're even thanked in the back." (Which they are, along with a hundred other people, including those who did real labor on the book, editing and proofreading and so on, as well as people who inspired me, even when in some cases I don't know them personally.) The drummer seems almost touched, at first. He introduces himself.

"Matt," he says.

"Duke," I say. I know I should leave it at that, but I keep talking. As I say, something isn't right with my brain. I don't linger *too* long, but in a transaction like this one, it's best to be as brief as possible.

"We'll read it," he tells me. I hate the sound of that "we." It sounds so impersonal, as if he knows I want the others to read the book as well, which I do, but still, who wants to feel like part of a targeted group instead of just himself?

I walk back to Bryce and the girls.

"I'm an idiot," I say. "I fucked it all up."

"Noooooooooo," say the girls, meaning it, as girls, bless their hearts, often do by way of consolation.

"You're just saying that," I say, knowing they're only consoling me.

The girls want to hang out. I can't hang out. I have to wake up early to rehearse my reading. Plus, I have to run around maniacally to collect a PA and set up the space and work out various other problems. This is a haphazardly organized reading.

I'm inclined to go back to my car and go home and sleep, but somehow I'm talked into getting into Bryce's car. There's no good reason for this, except one of the girls is insisting that Bryce will drive each of us to our respective cars, even though mine is parked only three blocks away.

So Bryce drops off the first of the girls, and I get out of his car to tell her good night. Then he drops me off at my car and drives away, and I make for home and, while I'm stopped at a traffic light, I check to see if I've gotten any text messages or the like, and realize I'm missing my phone. I know I had it outside the El Rey, because I checked it there as well. I pull over and search my car. The phone is definitely MIA. I drive back to where my car was parked and look around on the sidewalk. Not there. It must have fallen out of my pocket in Bryce's car, I decide, but I have no way of calling him.

But maybe I can call my own phone from a pay phone, and he'll hear it ring and stop and find it. Then I realize that won't work, since I stupidly set my phone to vibrate earlier in the evening.

I drive to Bryce's house. He's not there. I scribble a message and post it on his door, telling him to call me on my landline as soon as he gets home. Then, at my place, I try to call a few people to see if they have Bryce's number. I don't have it, since it's only on my phone.

Nobody picks up. It's after one in the morning after all.

So now I sit, waiting to see if Bryce is going to call before sunrise, and if he doesn't, I guess I'll have to cancel my phone service and buy a new phone. Except I can't buy a new phone, not right away, because I'm so broke I have to work at a pizzeria, where I'm probably going to get fired anyway; and I need to speak to a hundred people first thing in the morning about my reading, and I don't have half their numbers, which are all in my phone; and I don't even have a working alarm clock anymore, because I've come to use my phone as my alarm clock; and I could conceivably have lost my phone not in Bryce's car but in the spot where the first girl got out of his car and I got out to say good night, and I tried to search that spot but it was too dark to see; and somebody from Australia, say, might stumble on my phone and decide to call friends in Australia before I cancel my service, and I'll be liable for the bill; and Bryce is probably getting busy with the girl who insisted that I get into his car for no good reason, and he won't get the message I left on his door before that person from Australia has called everyone he knows Down Under and run up a $100,000 phone bill; and I made a fool of myself with Matt from the Walkmen, who's going to display my novel to his bandmates (if I'm lucky) and say, "Some psycho gave me this thing after you guys left last night"; and the reading is going to be even more disorganized than it would have been already; and here I sit, still waiting for Bryce to call, with no other way to pass the time than to write about my fucked night and ridiculous life.

But what the hell. Might as well post the results, right? My contributions to The Nervous Breakdown have mostly so far amounted to one of two topics: early death and personal embarrassment. Here's more of the latter. And seeing that I'm about to post without proofing, I may well have embarrassed myself further.

The perfect ending to a perfect day.

SAVED BY DEMON SONG

I'M HUNGRY. I have no money at all, none is expected soon, and there's no one from whom I can borrow any. I pace all night, wondering how to come by a few dollars to eat.

Finally, slowly, a plan unfolds: I can walk down the street to an ATM, fill out a deposit slip for a phantom check, feed the slip to the ATM, and request a cash advance. The bank, of course, will quickly discover that no check accompanied the deposit slip, but once I'm contacted, I'll simply say that, being in a hurry, I forgot. By then I hope to have thought of someone who's willing to cut me a bona-fide check.

If it works – if I manage to trick the ATM – it will only amount to a loan, or so I try to convince myself. The bank, on the other hand, could view it as fraud. I flash on stories of people imprisoned for stealing as little as five dollars, and can't decide if it's worth the gamble.

In the background I'm playing Nirvana's newly released *In Utero*, which I blast on my Walkman as I leave for the ATM at dawn. The music urges me on. It liquidates doubt and rallies me.

The ATM proves gullible.

I WAKE LATE after writing all night, and my roommate tells me that my car has been booted. I go to the window and look outside. Yes, my car has been booted. I owe close to $1,000 in unpaid parking tickets, and I have, at best, half that amount in my bank account. I return to bed, demoralized.

When I wake again, it's night. I'd been planning to see the Immortal Lee County Killers at Spaceland in Silver Lake, and I wait for my roommate to return home and possibly give me a ride, but he seems to be staying at his girlfriend's place. I decide to walk. It's a long walk, but, carless or not, I refuse to miss this band.

An empty cab passes me halfway to Silver Lake, and I hail it with a raised arm like the New Yorker I used to be. I'm surprised when it stops. I've never hailed a cab in L.A. before, I mention to the driver, who turns out to be a fellow expatriate New Yorker.

I ask what he thinks of L.A. He lists the usual complaints and asks what *I* think.

"Well," I say, "it's not New York, but it's got one thing going for it: every band in America plays here. You can't *not* play in L.A. And I've had a really fucked-up day, but I'm headed now to see a band, and I just know it's going to make me feel better."

It does. I walk home in a state of bliss.

I LEARN I won't be part of a band conceived to include me. There was no official announcement. Instead, I overhear a recording of a practice session, and a day later I'm invited to befriend the band on MySpace.

I take the news hard, prone on the sofa, crushed to the point of paralysis. It's partly – perhaps mostly – my fault that things developed as they did, and knowing that adds to the pain. It's physical pain. I feel as if I've swallowed poison.

I stare at my guitars, which rest on stands across the room. "Go on," I think, "pick one up." I finally do and sit on the floor and play a few chords. They suggest a melody, and I write a song in minutes. It seems to name itself: "You'll Find a Way."

I know I will. I have, many times, and I recognize the route by sound.

HAVE YOU SEEN MY HEAD?

AFTER ONE OF the first Die Princess Die shows I attended, Pete, the guitarist and co-frontman, asked what I thought. I allowed that the show was pretty good, except I wished the band would break more stuff. He considered that a lame reaction – or "stupid" is the adjective I believe he used. I was surprised, since we'd initially bonded over our shared enthusiasm for …And You Will Know Us by the Trail of Dead, a band notorious at the time for breaking stuff.

Over the next couple of years, however, Die Princess Die evolved into perhaps the most destructive, if not out and out violent, band in Southern California. They scared people, and I think that partly accounts for the large following they deserved but never acquired, despite having not just one but two frontmen with movie-star looks.

There was the show at the Echo, during which Danny, the drummer, hurled a cymbal that brained Bryce, the other guitarist/frontman. Bleeding like a diced pomegranate, Bryce was driven to the emergency room, where the gash on his skull was stapled shut.

There was the show at a downtown warehouse, during which Pete threw a tom that hit my hand and cut and nearly broke a finger. I nursed it with ice from the beer bin.

I was routinely one of Pete's targets. At another show at the Echo, he leaped off the stage and tackled me, and we wrestled on the floor as the crowd backed away. I won that bout but lost the rematch a few weeks later, when I realized my pants were falling off and I let Pete pin me before I mooned the bar. Strangers didn't realize Pete and I were friends. They thought it was a fight in earnest—which, in terms of effort, it was—and some were undoubtedly afraid of being attacked themselves.

But hipsters are a timid lot, for all their haughty airs, and that's especially true of the L.A. subspecies. It was different in San Diego, where DPD was formed; and one Friday night in the spring of 2005, I caught a ride to San Diego to see DPD play on its native turf, at a place called Scolari's Office.

It was, I noted immediately, a strange crowd: a mix of hipsters, hardcore punks, frat boys, longhairs, and even a few button-downed types who seemed to have wandered in for a nightcap. Pete was already half drunk at the bar, and we tossed back shots of whiskey as the first band played—a band featuring a wheelchair-bound paraplegic on guitar. That was a first, though I'd once caught a band with a one-legged guitarist who performed without a stool or crutches. Then, as our friend Dylan's band, the Great Escape, played its first show ever, I noticed that Ely, the DPD bass player, was behaving oddly. I asked somebody what was wrong with him and was told he'd been slipped a pill—a sedative of some kind. (San Diego has an inordinate amount of contraband pharmaceuticals, due to its proximity to Tijuana.) Ely could barely stand by the time DPD was about to go on, and he ended up playing on his back with his head hanging off the side of the stage. Except for his moving hands, he appeared to be unconscious.

Bottles were lobbed back and forth, some smashing near the bartender, who remained curiously indifferent. Soon the floor of the stage was covered with shards of glass, and Pete, cut, unwittingly splattered blood on the audience. A pair of longhairs, heads bobbing, called for further frenzy. They knew it was inevitable. They knew that DPD shows invariably ended in demolition, and they participated when the end came, heaving drums and guitars. Bryce, meanwhile, picked up a chair and hoisted it overhead, aiming for a table where the paraplegic was having a beer. I intervened, grabbing the chair before Bryce could throw it, finally managing to pry it loose as we circled round and round, both tugging.

It was over. Scolari's was spectacularly a mess, with cables looped everywhere, knotted around chairs and stools and even, I seem to recall, a light hanging low from the ceiling. Pete was missing a guitar. Bryce was missing a head. For a second, when he approached me and said as much, I thought he meant *his* head, but, no, he was referring to an amp head. I searched the bar, trying to help him find it, and saw a kid outside tapping on a traffic sign with Danny's stolen drumsticks. A girl was proudly displaying Pete's blood on her shirt. A homeless man was masturbating in the parking lot as people snapped photos on their phones.

I'm still amazed that we found our way to the prearranged crash pad. Only Pete knew the directions, and he'd all but passed out in the backseat.

"Which way?" we'd ask. "Pete? Left or right?"

"Left," he'd say, never raising his head.

"Are you sure?"

"Left, left. Go left."

He later threw up, and not having brought a change of clothes, he spent the next day sightseeing with his L.A. guests in puke-stained trousers.

I am writing at a moment when a great many people strike me as numbed to the point of catatonia. We live in a world of screens, hiding behind them, and we opt for mildly amusing "entertainment" over music or words or images that might cause us to feel something acute and therefore enduring. I'm guilty of the same. I've vegged in front of the TV and teared up over commercials while loathing myself for doing it; but I'm only human, and that's precisely what's exploited by marketing execs and the social scientists they hire to help them better apply the so-called human touch. This kind of cynicism breeds still more. It creates a kind of psychic plaque; a pollution of the soul.

Hence Die Princess Die and bands like them. There was purification in what some might dismiss as *actes gratuits*. They expressed what many sought and seek without knowing it.

I'm honored to have been their friend.

SUNSET ON SUNSET

PETE WANTED TO buy a guitar case for his Mexican-made acoustic. I, meanwhile, wanted to buy an acoustic of my own, as I mentioned one day when I dropped by Pete's apartment at the corner of McCadden and Willoughby. His living room was cluttered with amp heads, cabinets, and instruments in varying grades of disrepair. The beige carpet was speckled with stains, undoubtedly the result of spilled beer, and the retro sofa had slashes that, sealed with red tape, brought to mind wounds. Pete had drunkenly assaulted the sofa one night with a knife. The sofa had been bought by his ex.

He proposed that we go to Guitar Center, not far away on Sunset Boulevard. He didn't want to take his acoustic with him—it was too delicate, he said—so he laid it on a flattened cardboard box, traced it with a pen, and cut out a pattern to be used for measuring cases.

It was overcast and almost dusk, and Sunset sparkled with the headlights and tail lights of rush-hour traffic, as well as the lights of strip clubs, bars, and restaurants. We parked on a side street a block from Guitar Center, and walked past and over the handprints of music legends—Johnny Cash, Les Paul, Bo Diddley, and so on—in cement blocks surrounding the store's entrance. It was loud inside. It's always loud, as customers, usually guys, simultaneously noodle. I hate noodling. Once, shopping at Guitar Center, I played Johnny Ramone barre chords on a Fender Telecaster I coveted but couldn't afford, and noticed an employee bobbing his head in time to my riff. He must appreciate the change of pace, I thought.

Pete couldn't find a case upstairs, where new models are sold, so we went downstairs to the vintage room. He couldn't find a case there, either, and together we browsed the acoustics. One guitar fell within my price range, but Pete talked me out of buying it. I couldn't quite follow his reasoning, but, since he knew and knows more about guitars than I do, I took his advice.

We walked outside and went to another guitar store, a block away. There are a number of such stores on that stretch of Sunset, many selling vintage models only. Pete presented the pattern to the cashier: did he have a case that fit it? He didn't. We went to another store, darting across Sunset. Ordinarily, crossing Sunset in Hollywood triggers memories of being struck by a car near the present site of Amoeba Music, but that day I was happily reminded of playing hooky in middle school, when I'd blow off seventh period with my best friend Jay and head to his father's apartment beside a busy thoroughfare. I also flashed on my favorite shot in Oliver Stone's *The Doors*: a quick one of Val Kilmer, impersonating Jim Morrison, as he walks alone on Sunset at dawn, a flickering motel sign behind him. The movie could have easily done without that shot, and that it's gratuitous is, for me, one of its appeals. Then, too, it suggests something private about Morrison, who surely walked alone many times in Hollywood, occasionally detecting the scent of the miles-away ocean, as I could that day.

Pete and I went to store after store, but none of them had the case he wanted or an acoustic that perfectly suited me. I was drawn instead to the vintage electrics, as I always am, and every time I reached for one, I wondered who originally owned it and why it was sold to the next owner, and so on, until it hung, museumlike, on the wall of a store. Maybe the first owner was a novice whose lessons finally proved too expensive, and the second had a band that broke up when his girlfriend got pregnant, and the third pawned all his guitars, one by one, for drug money. My imagination tends toward the dramatic. Still, every used guitar for sale speaks to me of unfulfilled or exhausted aspiration, and so does every street in Los Angeles, which, at one time or another, is bound to have been traveled by a struggling musician, or an unemployed director, or a would-be actor whose name is lost to time. The rate of failure, compared to success, is obviously off the charts in L.A.

But the line between success and failure isn't as firm as I used to believe. I never bought a guitar that day, and Pete's pattern produced nothing, which is so often the case with patterns. And yet, when I leave L.A. for good one day—and I know I will—I'm sure I'll think fondly of walking on Sunset at sunset, failing to find what I came to find, like so many before me, not to mention the many trapped in traffic as far as I could see, their headlights and tail lights adding to a mood they likely failed to savor.

DEATH OF A UNICORN

I MET ALISON at a Die Princess Die show in May 2006. Our mutual friend Christopher introduced us. "You'll really hit it off," he said. "You both write about music." He and Alie and their friend Rhadeka had driven up from Santa Barbara, where they all lived, to see another band, but they stayed at my insistence for DPD. Alie liked them, as any true fan of rock & roll would, and after the show, she posted a comment on their MySpace page: *a swarm of razor blade butterflies to the face. fuck yeah.* She was spot-on—DPD *did* sound like a swarm of razor blade butterflies to the face—but her face was lightly scarred, so in that way her metaphor was disconcerting. I never asked Alie about the scars. I never asked her about her past, period, knowing through Christopher that she was in recovery, and not wanting to cause her discomfort.

Throughout the summer of 2006, we sporadically corresponded. I saved all her messages. Were we flirting? Maybe a little, to keep things interesting. In July we met downtown one night to see, among other bands, the Pope; and in August she wrote: *christopher, rhadeka and i are all going to tangier tonight for bryan's reading. can you go? it'd be nice to see you and you can check my new bleach blonde hair AND my new unicorn tattoo.*

Bryan, a poet, was another mutual friend. I drove to Tangier, where I first ran into Christopher, who told me that Alie and Rhadeka were ex-

cited about seeing me. "They *really* like you," he said. Alie looked great.
She had indeed bleached her hair white, though I don't remember seeing
her tattoo. Nor do I entirely remember my actions that night, but there's
a clue in the comment she posted the next day on my MySpace page: *aggressive hugs and aggressive jokes. all my other friends humor and affection is
total pussy bullshit now. thanks a lot.* My friend Sarah teased me about that
comment, referring to me as "bully boy."

A week later I did a reading from my novel, and invited Alie, who
responded late: *i was washing dishes at the cafe where i work during your
reading. but don't worry - i pictured it in my mind.*

That September, she published a piece in *Skyscraper* magazine, which
also featured an interview, conducted by someone else, with DPD. I had
recently published a piece about DPD in *Big Wheel*, a zine that now exists
only online, and I gave a copy to Alie when I met her and Rhadeka for
coffee at a Silver Lake Starbucks. At one point she mentioned that she
didn't like spending time in L.A. after her tumultuous history there – an
obvious allusion to her alcoholism, and the only one, to me at least, she
ever made. Still, that was as much as she said, and I didn't push for more,
again not wanting to cause her discomfort. I invited her to the Echo the
following week to see DPD, but she wrote back: *so i cant make it on sunday - but ill be in town on the 7th of october. i read your stuff in big wheel.
you're funny…* On another occasion she wrote: *when are we starting our
magazine?*

But she was moving to San Francisco, or so she said when we had coffee in September, and I figured that, once she moved, I'd probably never
see her again. She last wrote to me on November 10, 2006:

dearest duke,

the pope is playing on monday at the il corral. apparently they are
also playing christmas day at the north pole. but i think it would

be better if we just planned on going to the l.a. show, because getting a flight to [the] north pole on christmas can really be a bitch.

-alie

I ended up seeing another band that night with my friend Pete. Alie
called me, and I failed to call her back, though I did write to apologize.
She never replied, and a month later, checking MySpace one morning, I
found this message, posted by Rhadeka, on the bulletin board:

To All Friends of the Beautiful Aliebeth (aka Alison Meeder)

Alison passed away yesterday. She had been unreachable by phone
or e-mail since Tuesday, so last night three of us who speak with
her daily went to her house to make sure she was okay. We found
her in her bedroom.

Alison was a smart, beautiful, and, as we all know, hysterically
funny woman. She was also a severe alcoholic. After one year of
sobriety she began drinking again, and tragically did not make it
through this last binge. I am doing everything I can to keep the
image of the sarcastic unicorn-loving beautiful girl in my head, because the person I saw last night was not our Aliebeth.

Alie, I hope you are at peace, and I bet there are all kinds of heavy
metal unicorns where you are now.

She was twenty-seven years old. Her MySpace page still exists. It says
that she last checked in on December 12, 2006. It announces her current
age as thirty. Her "default image" is of a robot and a robotic-looking unicorn standing side by side in a heavenly mist. Robots, in theory, don't
die. Unicorns never existed. And why the fascination with unicorns in
the first place? At one time, I would've taken a Freudian approach: horses

were associated with masculinity – that is, strength – in ancient Greece, and the addition of a horn seems obviously phallic. But horses are fragile. Without human intervention – and even then – a fractured leg can easily prove fatal. A predator attacking a fleeing herbivore will often go for the legs, aiming to maim it. The imaginary horn supplies a defense otherwise lacking.

So Alie's choice of symbols have come with time to make sense to me. Her early death has not.

THE WORST CRIME

A DESPAIRING FRIEND called late one night to say that he was looking at a photo of himself as a toddler holding his father's rifle.

"I have an appointment with that rifle," he told me. "I've always known I was going to end my life with it."

He's fine now, thank God, but his remark brought to mind a journal entry I made as a teenager, in which I said that I was sure I was going to kill myself one day; it was only a matter of how and when.

I trashed that journal in my early twenties, embarrassed by my childish writing, thus symbolically killing the boy who wrote of killing himself. Yet something of that boy, strangely resilient for one so fixed on self-annihilation, survived.

I KNOW A number of aging punks who, to this day, despise Kurt Cobain because, they say, he made punk palatable to the masses and so ruined it; but I loved Kurt Cobain, since the arrival of Nirvana seemed to promise an overhaul of the mainstream culture that, for better or for worse, had shaped me. I gorged myself on *Nevermind* in the spring and summer of '92, eager for Nirvana's follow-up album in a way that's hard to imagine a person in 2010 sweating a forthcoming record (or movie or, *mirabile dictu*, book) as he or she would the latest gadget from Apple, technology being the twenty-first-century rock star.

Finally, in the fall of '93, *In Utero* was released, and I rushed out to buy it, despite my usual poverty; and seven months later, Kurt Cobain was dead. I was then in the middle of a media blackout, depressed about a novel I was fruitlessly struggling to finish; and my Echo Park neighbor Meg—a Seattle native and fellow Nirvana fan—called and listened, oddly quiet, as I whined about my book, until she managed to insert that Kurt Cobain had killed himself.

"*What?* When?"

"They found him a few hours ago. I called my mom and said, 'Mom, would you and Dad *please* take some flowers to Kurt's house and leave them there for me?"

She choked back a sob when she said that; and later, when Courtney Love read Cobain's suicide note aloud to mourners at a vigil in Seattle Center, she could barely speak for sobbing. My knowledge of Love's hellcat theatrics predated her celebrity. I'd heard firsthand tales of scrapes and lacerating phone messages ("You *know* you were the ugliest girl in high school," one of the latter went in part), but hearing her break down on television, I forgave her everything, though I personally had nothing to forgive.

CONVENTIONAL WISDOM HOLDS suicide to be selfish and cowardly. I'm sure this is a view that extends far back, but I don't remember hearing it when I was growing up. The prevailing view then, at least in my native Virginia, was of suicide as irredeemable sin. But the notion of sin no longer exists for many. To sin is to offend God, the ultimate authority. We're now more concerned with the offense done to ourselves.

Meanwhile, the current age—the age of überconsumerism and omnipresent, peekaboo screens—strikes me as selfish and cowardly indeed, so maybe it's a matter of the pot and the kettle, or, as Freud might have it, projection. As for me, I never sweepingly saw suicide as cowardly or selfish. I understand its legacy, and I'm sympathetic to the near and dear forced to live with it; but every choice is idiosyncratic, including the choice to die, and I try to bear in mind that I'm never going to know everything I'd need to know in order to judge.

In fact, I'm friendly with a woman who attempted suicide, and when I told her I couldn't judge her for it, she cried because so many *had* judged her for it. And why did she attempt suicide? Because she'd decided she was a poor excuse for a mother, and felt her children deserved better—how selfish is that?

And how selfish is this? In 1940, a catcher for the Cincinnati Reds named Willard Hershberger became the only baseball player ever to kill himself during the regular season. Here's an account from *Diamonds in the Rough*, a history of the game by Joel Zoss and John Bowman:

> Talented and well liked, Hershberger had descended into a deep melancholia that included insomnia, extended periods of depression, headaches, brooding over team losses, and fears that his teammates disliked him; he even told manager Bill McKechnie that he was going to kill himself. McKechnie became alarmed the next day when Hershberger failed to turn up as promised between games of a doubleheader with the Boston Bees, and dispatched businessman Dan Cohen, who was traveling with the team, to see what had become of him. Cohen discovered that Hershberger had spread towels on the bathroom floor, removed his shirt, and slit his throat as neatly as possible into the bathtub.
>
> [...] Hershberger's father had killed himself in a considerably bloodier fashion with a shotgun in the family bathroom when his son was eighteen years old and, as the psychologists say, young Willard probably felt responsible for a death he did not understand. His response—the morbid fear of disappointing people,

which helps explain his vow never to marry while his mother was alive—was manifest in an abnormal sense of responsibility that left him unable to forgive himself once he determined that he had let his teammates down. He even tried to mitigate the mess he knew his death would make by spreading towels on the bathroom floor.

For somebody selfish, he was nothing if not considerate. Meanwhile, here's the unfortunate coda:

Mr. Cohen, the man who discovered [Hershberger's] body, later committed suicide, too.

As I said, I do understand the legacy. Suicide appears to be something of a meme, which explains its occurrence in clusters, and renders it a subject largely avoided, particularly in thanataphobic America.

FOR A LONG time after Kurt Cobain's death, I couldn't listen to Nirvana, since Cobain's final act, I thought, was tantamount to saying that he wanted to be forgotten. It was too painful, anyway, to hear fraught lyrics like "I don't have a gun" from "Come as You Are," a song I used to love.

Then, one night three years ago, I was at my friend Pete's place, watching TV with Pete and his roommate, Larry, who asked if we'd seen the DVD included in the Nirvana box-set retrospective, *With the Lights Out*. I hadn't, and Larry played it, and the Nirvana magic revived. Our friends Wade and Bryce dropped by, pulling up chairs without a word. Some clips we watched repeatedly, and afterward we talked about the impact that Nirvana, and Cobain specifically, had on each of us.

"He's what caused me to become a musician," Larry said. "I saw Nirvana and told my parents, 'I know what I want to do now.'"

"I stopped listening to *my* parents," Pete said. He also read a Cobain biography—one of just two books he claims to have read from start to finish. He loaned me his copy of the bio before I left that night, and I've yet to return it. But I still can't bring myself to listen much to Nirvana.

DURING ONE OF many troubled periods in my life, I saw a psychotherapist who told me that suicide has to do with "a loss of self," citing, by way of example, the stock-market crash of 1929, when former millionaires, paupers overnight, allegedly killed themselves in droves. The sudden poverty, my therapist explained, wasn't the cause so much as what it spelled in terms of identity: if I'm not a millionaire, then who am I?

Or maybe the cause isn't a loss of self so much as self-surfeit. Mary Richert, another contributor to The Nervous Breakdown, once noted, in a blog entry, her wariness of first-person narrative, in part because, if I recall correctly, she heard or read that people with a fondness for the word "I" are the ones most inclined to kill themselves. Elsewhere, I've encountered arguments for first-person narrative as "problematic," and while I forget the reasoning, I think it usually boils down to a distaste for egotism.

By contrast, I find third-person narrative problematic. Only God is omniscient–if, that is, God exists. Meanwhile, I don't see how anyone can write without egotism, as the Internet corroborates, with so many opinions expressed–*too* many, to express still another opinion. The Tower of Babel has been built anew.

Obviously, there's no single cause of suicide, which isn't always accomplished decisively, in a conscious act. People court death in myriad ways–unhealthy habits, reckless hobbies, dangerous occupations–and they aren't tallied as suicides when the Reaper responds to his summons. I once dropped acid and sped around Manhattan on a motorcycle. Later, dodging traffic in Los Angeles, I was mowed down by a car. Still later, I snorted heroin while smashed on alcohol–a dicey combination–though the first time I did it, I was unaware of the risk, and the second time, I thought I was snorting coke, not heroin. Even so, in reflecting on that occasion, and numerous others, I recognize that I was inadvertently suicidal.

For the most part, though, when the abyss beckoned, I think I was fully cognizant of it, and never much for secrecy, I confided in friends. Some hotly told me never to speak of such things, effectively ending the conversation. Others recommended psychotropic drugs, which I refused to consider, unwilling to live – around the clock, at least – in a chemical haze. Still others patronized me. People who kill themselves, I was lectured, don't talk about it beforehand; they just do it.

In fact, the opposite is usually true, though the warnings are frequently ignored. I heard of one such case, as reported by someone present: a young actor named Jonathan Brandis, a regular on the nineties TV show *SeaQuest* and depressed about his subsequent career, announced to friends at a gathering at his place that he was going to hang himself. He even showed them the rope: "Do you think this will work?" "Yeah, Jonathan, that'll work just fine." Then he disappeared, and finally someone decided to see where he'd gone – too late.

This story may have been distorted in the telling, but it serves a point. Jonathan's friends thought he was seeking attention, and there are certainly those who speak of suicide for that reason, but even they should be taken seriously.

Have *I* ever spoken of suicide by way of seeking attention? Probably. But that doesn't mean I wasn't in a lot of pain.

I'm not in that kind of pain at the moment. To put it more plainly, this is not a suicide note, though I've written one or two.

KURT COBAIN'S SUICIDE note suggests, in some ways, a Willard Hershberger mind-set. Cobain writes of feeling "guilty beyond words" for his failure to experience "the excitement of listening to as well as creating music along with reading and writing for too many years now." The mention of reading is curious, but no matter; Cobain seems to feel he's disappointing people, as he fairly explicitly states in the note's most famous passage:

> The fact is, I can't fool you, any one of you. It simply isn't fair to you or me. The worst crime I can think of would be to rip people off by faking it and pretending as if I'm having 100% fun.

When Courtney Love read that bit aloud at the Seattle vigil, she interjected, "No, Kurt, the worst crime *I* can think of is for you to just continue being a rock star when you fucking hated it. Just fucking *stop*."

Near the end of the note, almost as famously, Cobain writes:

> I'm too much of an erratic, moody baby! I don't have the passion anymore, and so remember, it's better to burn out than to fade away.

Those who regard suicide as inherently selfish and cowardly must surely approve of Cobain's self-characterization as "an erratic, moody baby." Meanwhile, "it's better to burn out than to fade away" is a lyric from the Neil Young song "Hey Hey, My My (Into the Black)," which references Johnny Rotten, who, fed up with being a Sex Pistol, iconically sat onstage during the last show of the Pistols' landmark American tour and said to the audience, "Ever get the feeling you've been cheated?"—a remark similar in spirit to Cobain's notion of "the worst crime." Johnny Rotten left the Pistols the following day and went on to start Public Image Ltd., a band free of the controversy, and resulting media melee, that guaranteed a hellish ride for the Pistols.

Courtney Love was right. If Cobain hated being a rock star, he could have—and should have—stopped. He lacked the temperament to weather fame, unlike his wife. He was "too sensitive," as he writes in the note, though his music was often aggressive—a dichotomy at the heart of his appeal. I see that dichotomy in myself – and I'm not the only one, as Cobain sang in "Rape Me." He wasn't a Gen X hero for nothing.

Of course, no one knows what was going through his mind before he pulled the trigger – including, I'd venture, Cobain himself – but I can't believe he really wanted to die. I don't believe *I* ever wanted to die when I was feeling suicidal. Rather, it was *my life* I wanted to destroy, and by that I mean all those elements in my life that felt and feel like death: the grind of poverty and Sisyphean labor; the demands of people who feel like so many pecking starlings; the sense that something deep in my soul, which Nietzsche defined as a "stomach," isn't being fed, or – another stab at saying the same thing – I look for fire and find mostly ash.

We die in increments before we die altogether. We fade away, to return to the note and Neil Young's lyric. There's no getting around it, but it's a matter of degree, I think. Passion doesn't have to perish, though it doubtlessly comes under a great deal of attack; and some lose the will to defend it, if they ever had the will – or passion itself – to begin.

I did, and by the grace of God I've reclaimed it – again and again and again. That's what it takes to stay alive, and I want so very much to live.

IV. FAMA

FRIDAY BLOODY FRIDAY

WHEN I WAS about to publish *Banned for Life*, I had a number of exchanges with Jonathan Evison, an acclaimed writer whose counsel I sought with regard to promotion, among other matters. He was aware of certain aspects of my past, and he advised me to be forthcoming about them, since to do otherwise, he said, would amount to breaking faith with readers.

Jonathan is a wise man, but I regarded *Banned* as my child, and so wanted to shield it from the sins of its father. I imagined dismissive reviews based less on the book and more on my rap sheet, as well as sneering remarks posted on message boards. Paranoia? But I've been the target of such remarks, and I wanted to give *Banned* a running start before I fell on my sword.

Now, I figure, the time has come. *Banned* has barely been noticed since it appeared more than six months ago, and I've tested the waters with friends made since, and none have responded as feared.

So ready the rotting fruit, as St. Francis of Assisi might have said before stripping in public, and cue the flashback ripple effect.

A LITTLE OVER twenty years ago, I was an actor living in Williamsburg, Brooklyn. There weren't many actors living in Williamsburg at the time, but I considered myself an unusual case: a hip kid (I would never have copped to being a "hipster"), as opposed to my colleagues, who overwhelmingly struck me as squares. The most happening neighborhood in New York was the Lower East Side, and that's where I was usually found, raising hell with the likes of my friend Morphine, whose nickname somehow owed to his slamdancing days at punk clubs such as A7. I studied with Mira Rostova, a creased but still-beautiful Russian who'd famously coached Montgomery Clift, and did a lot of fringe theater – a far-out staging of *Richard II*, for instance, in which the actors, cast in multiple roles, carried leather masks to designate which role was being played. You'd have to ask the director why we carried the masks instead of wearing them. I never did understand.

One spring night, recovering at home after dropping acid with Morphine, I got a call from a film director who was in L.A. to make a movie for Roger Corman, and my director friend wanted to know if I could board a plane immediately to star in it. I'd appeared in one of the director's student shorts at NYU, and Corman had given him carte blanche in the casting department. The movie, he explained, had no screenplay, even though production was slated to begin in a couple of days. Corman, the so-called King of the Bs, was known for rushing projects into production in order to make use of standing sets at his converted-lumberyard studio. No screenplay? Take the weekend to write one and report to the set first thing Monday.

Well, of course I flew to L.A., where I was met at the airport by a production assistant whose car promptly broke down on the freeway. A symbol of things to come? Yes, it would seem. This was obviously before cell phones, so we hiked till we found a pay phone, after which another production assistant drove us to Roger Corman's office. I'd seen Corman in-

terviewed many times on television, and knew he'd launched, among
others, Jack Nicholson and Robert DeNiro; and I hoped to be next. I resolved to have as much input as possible in the way my part was written.

Here I'd like to note that I was a serious, if uncredentialed, student of
literature. I read so much, in fact, that one of my exes used to complain
that I spent all my money on booze and books, which inconveniently
couldn't be bought at the same locations. At any rate, I left Corman's office for a Mexican restaurant with the director and the screenwriter, and
within a few hours I'd arranged to have the screenwriter fired. He was too
plodding, too conventional, and none of his ideas jibed with mine. The
director and I collaborated on the screenplay together – or we did before
I took over the writing alone. It helped, of course, that Roger liked me.
I was told by one of his assistants that I put him in mind of himself as a
young man. I was certainly ambitious, as my ruthless behavior indicates.

One day, between takes on the set, Roger announced that he wanted
me to write another movie for him. I wasn't interested. I wanted to establish myself as an actor, not a screenwriter, and people have a terrible way
of insisting that you're one thing or the other. Renaissance men are anach-
ronistic. We live, and have for some time, in an age of specialization.

But people told me I was being foolish. This was a great opportunity,
they said. I had a chance to earn my keep by writing – a chance denied so
many others. I decided to go forward, thinking I could create more parts
for myself, not realizing that most directors would cast anyone *but* the
writer. An old Hollywood saying applies: a screenwriter on a set is like a
whore sticking around for breakfast.

So I remained in L.A. after production wrapped, sniffing opportunity, and took an apartment on Beachwood Drive, in the shadow of the
Hollywood sign. My Virginia driver's license had lapsed during my time
in New York, so I couldn't drive; and since I couldn't yet afford a phone,
I'd head numerous times daily to a pay phone outside the Beachwood

Market. And it was there, on that corner, on that phone, that I learned that someone at Paramount, based on fast-traveling reports of my work at Corman, wanted to hear my ideas for the latest *Friday the 13th* sequel.

IF I WAS snobby about books—and I was: no guilty pleasures—I was equally snobby about films. In New York I haunted the art houses, where I'd sometimes tangle with other snobs, arguing the merits of this auteur over that one. Horror movies, which I'd liked in my early teens, were irrelevant as far as I was concerned, so I was only dimly aware of the *Friday the 13th* phenomenon, which seemed to involve witless fornicators being subjected to unsought surgery by a hulking mute in a hockey mask. No thanks.

Still, never thinking I'd get the job, I rented every *Friday* movie and watched them on a neighbor's VCR. I'd been told that the *Friday* producers had wanted Jason Vorhees, the hulking mute, to square off in the seventh *Friday* with Freddy Krueger, the razor-fingered pickle of the *Nightmare on Elm Street* series, and though the deal had (for the moment) fallen through, a variation was desired. I had the formula down by the end of *Part 2* at least, and I walked to the Beachwood Market pay phone and called the *Friday* development person and pitched her my ideas. No, she said to each one. Uh-uh. No, that's not for us. On the phone, she struck me as a mythical creature incredibly proving to be real: the hard-as-nails, bottom-line Hollywood exec, as encapsulated in the back-cover copy of airport novels. I shuddered at the idea of having to deal with more of her kind. I never had in New York, aside from casting directors, who on occasion revealed traces of mammalian warmth.

Then I came to an idea she liked. She proposed that we get together, and a few days later I walked to her office on the Paramount lot, where she was finishing a meeting with another writer: a lauded playwright who was working on a script for a drama featuring Keanu Reeves, whose star was just beginning to unaccountably rise. The furniture in the office was universally white. The receptionist, waitresslike, offered me a bottle of water. I watched the playwright leave in a bit of a huff, and the development person at last emerged to welcome me.

"He's annoyed," she said of the playwright, "because we told him to change the script, and now we told him to change it all back." She laughed. In person she didn't seem hard at all, but her laughter was unsettling. "Aren't my whims amusing?" it seemed to say. "Today I want it in red, and tomorrow I'll want it in green, and who knows how I'll want it the day after that?"

In fact, once the job was mine, she would change her mind repeatedly. By then I'd moved to a house in Silver Lake, where I camped on the porch, and when I wasn't writing, I'd drink with friends, usually sleeping late and often woken by a call from Paramount. Can you come over and meet with us? We're not happy with the last draft. I was working on two scripts at the time – the second was for Roger – but I didn't have a computer and the *Friday* people did, and they wanted new drafts *immediately*. This meant that after the meeting, which involved sheaves of detailed notes, I'd be extradited to a trailer on the lot, where I was expected to produce a page-one rewrite by the start of the following day. Then I'd return home and crash and, two days later, get another call from Paramount, and head with a hangover to the lot and bang out another draft.

Some nights, treating myself to a break, I would roam the sleeping lot, imagining the greats who might have worked on this stage or that one. W.C. Fields, the Marx Brothers, Marlene Dietrich, Carole Lombard, Gary Cooper, Rudolph Valentino, Edward G. Robinson, Mae West, William Holden: all made movies at Paramount. Of course, nowadays people don't care about any of them. Not that they cared much in the late eighties.

I also read letters from *Friday* fans, which were tacked to the bulletin board in the trailer where I worked, and struck up a correspondence with an Ohio teenager whose letter was precociously clever. I thought he'd appreciate hearing from the writer of the forthcoming sequel, but he didn't—not particularly—and the correspondence soon ended. Still other letters, undisplayed, were described to me as cries for help from kids claiming to have been permanently traumatized by Jason Vorhees. I could sympathize, having had panic attacks in my teens that were induced, in part, by violent movies. Now I was writing one. Go figure.

I PROBABLY PRODUCED around fifteen drafts for *Friday the 13th Part VII*, when I was contracted for four. My agent decided I should get more money, and contacted the *Friday* producers, who responded by hiring another writer for the final tweaks. This writer, whom I never met, used a pseudonym, which I should've done also. That I didn't is something of a mystery to me. I think I had an idea that a pseudonym would be dishonest and cowardly. Plus, I didn't take the movie at all seriously, and I figured my amused attitude toward it would be shared by others. We all do silly things, I thought, especially in our salad days. Surely people would cut me slack.

So I foolishly put my name on the movie and only started using a pseudonym later, after the Internet Movie Database had oozed from the river Styx and my every embarrassing credit could be, and was, accessed. The years after *Friday* weren't kind ones. I was nearly killed when a car struck me in a Hollywood crosswalk, and I had numerous surgeries to reconstruct an arm and leg, which triggered the return of the panic attacks that had scrambled my brain as a kid. I was dumped by my agent and, unable to find another, relied on word of mouth for work, and some of the results made *Friday* look like *The Battleship Potemkin*. I continued to act, but movies in general had gotten so bad, and my so-called writing career had indeed hurt my prospects as an actor: are you a writer who acts, or an actor who writes? I felt more and more like an interloper – certainly a renegade. I barely socialized with industry people. I went underground, living as I had in New York, hanging with musicians and bohemians of all stripes, and almost never mentioned how I paid the rent.

Yet people knew. Movies would turn up on TV, prompting shocked phone calls: "Why didn't you *tell* me you were an actor?" I wasn't so easily Googled, since my new friends knew me by the nickname I'd acquired after the accident (Duke, short for Iron Duke, which refers to the titanium that holds my shattered limbs together), but they learned that I was a screenwriter as well as an actor; I was never sure how. I was friendly with …And You Will Know Us by the Trail of Dead, for instance, a band that appears in *Banned for Life*, and while they were on tour in Australia, they posted a message at their Yahoo! group, to which I belonged, asking which *Friday* movie I'd written. This led to a flurry of messages from other group members: "Did you write the sleeping-bag kill? That's my favorite *Friday* kill ever!" I was, for a fact, responsible for the sleeping-bag kill, though I was unaware of its iconic status.

Meanwhile, elsewhere on the Internet, some geek accused me of stealing that scene from a movie unknown to me. I was routinely attacked online, particularly after I gave a couple of interviews in which I spoke about my *Friday* experience in appropriately negative terms. Somebody said I should die for that – "with a red-hot poker up [my] ass." Still others, on seeing some other horrible movie I was forced to take because I was broke, would spare the director (and producer and cast and so on) and blame *me* for the movie, based on my de-facto resume at IMDb. It was bound be my fault, what with the stuff I'd done. But I was only doing what I was told to do – what I *had* to do in order to get paid. I probably would've been better off with a so-called real job, but I was an exceedingly poor candidate for one after being out of the market for so long. Funds would dwindle, and I'd scramble for a writing job before my landlords hit me with a Pay Or Quit notice, and I always managed to find one – or I did until recently. I've now written more than twenty feature-length produced screenplays, which is quite a record, though I'm in no way proud of it, and a few of the movies turned out okay. The best of the lot may be *Life Among the Cannibals*, a black comedy in which I had a prominent role as a serial killer. It never received any distribution in the U.S., though it won a couple of awards at film festivals.

As Brando, whose heir I once aspired to be, said in *On the Waterfront*: I could've been a contender. Instead of a bum. Which is what I am.

WELL, PERHAPS NOT entirely. In 2000, while on location for a film in Belgrade, I came up with the idea for *Banned for Life* and remained in Belgrade after production wrapped to work on the book, returning to the States with a first draft. Then, for years, I refined and polished, hoping to establish, once and for all, that I had talent, that I'd been badly served by the movies, that I deserved to be taken seriously.

Ironically, I didn't feel I could put my name on *Banned*. I'd destroyed my name, or so I thought. At the same time, it would've killed me to use a pseudonym. How could I use a pseudonym on a work so close to my heart?

Some suggested that I call myself Duke Haney, but my nickname could be learned on IMDb. So, in the end, I became D.R. Haney; and to further distance myself from my actor-screenwriter identity, I submitted a report of my death (by heroin overdose) to IMDb. They required proof, so I doctored my Wikipedia bio, which was soon corrected by a meddling stranger. Enraged, I deleted the bio, but yet another meddling stranger restored it. I don't know why I have a Wikipedia bio in the first place. I don't warrant one.

In any case, IMDb never reported me as dead. I hate IMDb. It's full of inaccuracies—an ex-girlfriend, for instance, is erroneously said there to be the daughter of Bobby Kennedy—but the world regards it as *the* authority. Meanwhile, this all goes to show how desperate I was to hide my past.

But no more. I've done what I've done. And now I'm free to tell stories I couldn't tell before, since to do so would've been to give myself away. And I am bloody well going to tell them.

Oh, yes. There's much to tell.

"FARRAH! YOU'RE BEAUTIFUL! I LOVE YOU!"

I WAS A teenager living in New York. George was my brilliant roommate, and sometimes, if we weren't doing anything, one of us would say, "Do you want to walk aimlessly around?" That was our standard joke. But we did, for a fact, spend much time walking aimlessly all over Manhattan, and one early-winter night on the Upper East Side, far from the hovel we shared near the Williamsburg Bridge, there were flashbulbs popping on the sidewalk ahead of us. A celebrity must be near—a celebrity being hounded by the paparazzi. We got closer and saw that the celebrity was Farrah Fawcett.

She looked great, of course. She looked like Farrah Fawcett, only more so. She was standing on a corner and being apparently interviewed by a man with a small tape recorder as a couple of shutterbugs circled her, snapping photos. I hadn't been in New York very long, so I was unaccustomed to seeing famous people, and I blurted out: "Farrah! You're beautiful! I love you!"

She turned to me and laughed with that famous, toothy, openmouthed Farrah smile and said, "Thanks." She instantly struck me as a good egg.

George and I kept walking, and I stopped and decided to ask for an auto-graph for my younger brother and sister. Honestly, it wasn't for me. I was an uncouth kid slightly awed by fame, but I cared nothing about auto-graphs. I found a pen and searched my pockets for a piece of paper, and all I could produce was a dollar bill. That would have to suffice.

I walked back, toward Farrah, who was still on the corner being inter-viewed by the man with the tape recorder, and thought, "Oh, leave the poor woman alone. She's got enough problems with all these media peo-ple." I paused, about to turn and walk away, but Farrah had seen me, and she clearly knew what I had in mind.

"Come here," she said, again smiling. She said this as if she were a small-town beauty queen who was sitting in a booth selling kisses for a dollar and I'd paid the dollar but was now too shy to collect, and she, who was used to such shyness, which she seemed to regard as charming, was gently chiding me for losing my nerve.

I walked over with the pen and dollar bill and handed them to her. I, too, was now being photographed by the paparazzi. She was wearing brown knitted gloves, I remember, that matched her light-brown suede jacket. She smelled like heaven. She glanced at the dollar bill and said, "Don't you have anything else?"

I shook my head.

"Oh, well," she said, and she asked me to turn around, and she pressed the dollar bill against my back, and I felt the tip of the pen as she wrote something. I can feel it now as I write these words.

I thanked her and walked off with George and glanced at the dollar bill. In one corner of it, near the portrait of George Washington, she'd written, in cursive lettering I recognized from one of her celebrated post-ers, "Love, Farrah." I presented the dollar bill to my brother, David, and my sister, Dawn, when I went home to Virginia for Christmas. They were delighted, though perhaps not quite as delighted as I expected.

Years passed. All of this was more or less forgotten. Then one night, as I was having a beer with David, something brought it back to me.

"Hey," I said, "whatever happened to that dollar bill with Farrah Fawcett's autograph?"

"Dawn spent it."

"She *did*?"

"Yeah, she really wanted to buy a Coke, and that was the only money she had."

It made sense, in a way. A portrait of George Washington, autographed by one of Charlie's Angels, spent on a Coke in a Virginia store. What could possibly be more American?

Your kindness warms me still, Farrah.

THE RIGHT PROFILE

I DON'T KNOW where I got the idea that I could act, but I always assumed I could. When I was ten I wrote a play about an Indian massacre and talked my school into staging it, claiming the lead role – an Indian chief – for myself. A year later I wrote a Christmas play to be performed for hospitalized children and, slackening on my star trip, took a supporting part as one of Santa's elves. (I was the German elf, since I had Santa's workshop as a kind of United Nations, with elves representing as many countries as there were classmates to be cast.) The one and only performance of that play was covered by my hometown paper, which naturally pleased my parents.

Then, for a while, I lost interest in acting. I despised theater kids, who'd burst into song by way of greeting, meantime flicking the scarves they uniformly wore. Also, theater acting was broad and embellished, unlike the intimate acting of movies. I loved movies. I always had. But as I dealt with the usual horrors of adolescence, movies took on new importance. I was touchy, mopey, and mad at the world for reasons I couldn't altogether verbalize. If I'd known about punk rock, I would surely have embraced it; but I didn't, not yet, and the only people who seemed to feel as I did were the ones I saw onscreen. I recognized myself when Jack Nicholson lashed out in *Five Easy Pieces*, which often played at the local repertory cinema. The same with Al Pacino in *Dog Day Afternoon*, another repertory-cinema constant, as was *Who'll Stop the Rain* with Nick Nolte, who at one point growled a line I've never forgotten: "All my life I've been taking shit from inferior people. No more."

Actors like Nolte, Pacino, and Nicholson helped me through a difficult time, but it never occurred to me that I could join them onscreen until the night I watched *They Shoot Horses, Don't They?* on television. It's a bleak movie that naturally appealed to my bleak state of mind, and halfway through, I thought, "Hey, why couldn't *you* be an actor?" "Because," I thought a minute later, "it's impossible." But *why* was it impossible? Other people did it, right? Then I went to the bathroom and stared at myself for a long time in the medicine-cabinet mirror, trying to decide if I had a face that was screen-worthy. I was fifteen and very uncomfortable with my appearance, but I tried to project ahead, adding years and lines and weight (I was a twig at fifteen), and if I aged as hoped—yes, I could picture myself onscreen.

It was one of the key moments of my life. Everything that's happened to me since can be traced to it. I resolved, then and there, that I was going to be an actor—a successful *movie* actor—and so I began to prepare.

Not that I took acting classes or did theater—not right away. In fact, I kept my resolution secret for some time, fearing ridicule. Only my best friend Jay knew, and when I told him, he decided to become a screenwriter, being as enamored of movies as I was. We made plans to leave Virginia as soon as we finished high school. I even had the route sketched out; we'd stop here the first night, and there the night after, and if we made good time, we should arrive in Los Angeles in as little as three days.

The idea of heading alone to L.A. scared me. It seemed so big, so foreign, so far away.

But Jay's interest in screenwriting was predictably facile, so our scheme to tag-team the movie world soon faded. Meanwhile, I was having doubts about L.A. I read constantly about the actors I admired, and most had gotten their starts in New York. I made notes about their schools and teachers, and sent away for literature about this program and that one. I learned that actors needed photographs in order to get work, and I asked my mother's boyfriend (now my stepfather), who was a professional photographer, to shoot some photos of me as an experiment, borrowing a friend's peacoat in lieu of the black leather jacket I wanted to wear but couldn't find.

But I mostly prepared by watching movies. I wanted to absorb the history of the art form. I wanted to study famous actors of the past. My tastes were very narrow in those days, so comedic actors made slight, if any, impact. The actors I most liked were associated with the kitchen-sink Method school, going back to John Garfield, who emerged from the Group Theater, from which the Actors Studio later sprang. Marlon Brando was associated with the Actors Studio, and Brando was the king of actors in my eyes. I'd never seen such raw emotion pour off the screen. At the same time, Brando was capable of elaborate impersonations, as most "primitive" actors aren't, just as actors with a gift for mimicry tend to hide behind it.

James Dean was a product of the Studio, but I had mixed feelings about Dean, who initially struck me as a Brando imitator. Now I can see that he had a style all his own, though he died before he could fully develop it. And then there was Montgomery Clift, who, despite his limited Studio dealings, was nonetheless classified as a Method actor. Brando, I knew, regarded Clift as his "touchstone" and rival, but I'd seen only a single clip of Clift, on a TV special one night. The clip was from *A Place in the Sun*–a love scene with Elizabeth Taylor–and Clift's brooding, intense, troubled persona left a deep impression. Then, too, like Brando and Dean, he was considered a rebel, which to me automatically raised his stock. As I've said, I was a punk rocker waiting to happen, and Brando and Dean especially had a huge impact on early punk fashion and attitude. As for Clift, he was the subject of the Clash song "The Right Profile," with lyrics that referenced the 1956 car crash that mangled Clift's looks.

It also mangled his already-precarious psyche. Some have said it marked the start of the longest suicide in Hollywood history, and even Marilyn Monroe once cited Clift as "the only person I know who's in worse shape than I am." They died four years apart, both alcoholics hooked on prescription drugs, which they were known to share. Of the three great rebel actors of the 1950s, only Brando survived to old age, and Clift is sadly neglected now; but thanks to a couple of recent biographies, he was enjoying a bit of a posthumous comeback around the time I met his brother.

MOST OF THE actors I admired were on record as preferring theater to film, and, intent on following them in every way, I figured I should start doing plays. Still, there weren't many opportunities locally, aside from high-school musicals and the snooty Virginia Players, so I applied for a six-week summer program with a theater company in Washington, D.C. The program included acting classes that would culminate in a one-off production. It was inexpensive. It was 120 miles from home and snickering peers. I worked to raise the necessary funds, crossing my fingers that I'd be accepted. I was, and I boarded a Greyhound for Alexandria, Virginia, where I'd booked a room at the YMCA.

I hadn't realized, before I arrived, just how far Alexandria was from Georgetown, where the company held classes. But no matter; I commuted every day by bus, occasionally seated next to punk rockers: my first exposure to them. We never exchanged a word. I wish, being curious, I'd braved a few. But I was laser focused on the business of becoming an actor, and especially obsessed with impressing one of my teachers: a New York native of the Method school.

One day, in the *Washington Post*, I read an article about Brooks Clift, Montgomery's brother, who lived in the D.C. suburbs and was married to the journalist Eleanor Clift, later famous as a regular on *The McLaughlin Group*. The article mentioned that, like Monty, Brooks had been an actor, as well as a TV director, and it touched on his unusual childhood, much of which had been spent in Europe, where he and his younger brother and sister were tutored in the ways of aristocracy, as dictated by their mother, Sunny. She was the unacknowledged granddaughter of Abraham Lincoln's Postmaster General, Montgomery Blair, whose father-in-law had served in two presidential cabinets in addition to sitting on the Supreme Court; and Sunny's vocation, never realized, was to see her children, as well as herself, welcomed into the Blair fold. (I would later come across a photograph of Montgomery Blair as a young man in a Civil War history, and his resemblance to his namesake great-grandson was eerily striking; but for the century that divided them, they might have been twins.)

I was fascinated by the *Post* article. I was sure I'd never get to meet Brando, and Dean and Clift were covered by grass, but the latter's brother – the next best thing – was living nearby and listed in the phone book, address included, as I happily discovered. Should I call and ask if he'd be willing to receive me? No, I decided; he'd probably decline. I charted the route to his house and, a day or so later, caught a series of buses to a comfortably middle-class neighborhood, where I saw three boys playing on the lawn of the two-storey Clift house. The oldest of the boys was maybe ten and, like the others, tow-headed. I paced past them a couple of times, uncertain of how to proceed.

Then one of the smaller boys spoke to me – I forget what he said – and I stopped pacing and spoke back. I was an acting student, I told him, and I'd read an article in the paper about his uncle. At that point the oldest boy took over, announcing with pride that his middle name was Montgomery.

"And *my* middle name is Blair," said one of the younger boys, not to be outdone.

I asked if their father was at home, and the oldest boy waved for me to follow him and ran inside and up the stairs, while I awkwardly waited by the open door. A second later he raced down the stairs and charged past me, into the yard. Then his father appeared, wearing shorts and dark-framed glasses. He didn't much resemble Monty, I thought, though they shared the same small-boned build and thick brows. He stumbled a bit, descending the stairs, and quickly sat on one of them – had he been drinking? But he was cogent when he spoke, and nothing about him, apart from his stumbling, suggested drunkenness. I apologized for intruding, explaining who I was and why I'd come. He was gracious. He enjoyed hearing from people with an interest in acting, he said. He asked about the classes I was taking and my plans for the future, and I told him I hoped to attend the Neighborhood Playhouse, a school in New York responsible for the likes of Robert Duvall. Brooks chuckled. He'd studied with Sanford Meisner, the Neighborhood Playhouse founder, but they never got along, since he, Brooks, had "refused to play the homosexual game."

"He doesn't have a voice," he added about Meisner.

"What do you mean?"

"He had throat cancer, and they had to remove his larynx. You know, I always noticed that people get cancer in the part of their bodies they use the most, and Sandy never stopped screaming."

In fact, when I later auditioned for the Neighborhood Playhouse, Meisner walked past, speaking with an electrolarynx. Brooks recommended a different teacher (not Mira Rostova, Monty's coach and, eventually, mine as well) and encouraged me to move to New York.

"It's a great city," he said. "You can go there and get a place, and nobody will ever bother you. People leave you alone there." I didn't understand what he meant by that, but I looked forward to the day I would.

Of course, we mostly spoke about his brother, since I'd described myself as a huge fan, despite knowing practically nothing about him. "What was he *like*?" I asked Brooks, whose first word in response was "Funny" – hardly the one I would've expected for the Byronic Montgomery Clift. (Note to self: it's okay to have a sense of humor.) He talked quite a bit about a certain Dr. Silverberg (I kept hearing "silver bird"), who was Monty's psychoanalyst, and so oddly, unprofessionally close to him (they even vacationed together) that some suspected sexual involvement.

"Most of Monty's friends didn't approve of Silverberg," Brooks said. "But I think, without him, Monty wouldn't have lasted as long as he did."

He invited me upstairs to a room where he kept his brother's belongings. The *Post* article had mentioned that he had the X-ray taken of Monty's skull on the night of the accident, which I morbidly hoped would be on display. It wasn't. The only belongings I saw were books.

"Do you read?" Brooks asked.

"Of course," I said, afraid I seemed illiterate.

"*What* do you read?"

"Um, like, you know, stuff about actors. Stuff about how to make it."

He shook his head dismissively.

"Monty read *everything*," he said, "and when he was preparing for a role, he'd go, 'Oh, it's like that book I just finished.' He was always making connections like that. And he was an expert in the subject of psychology. He'd read all of Freud, so when he actually came to play Freud, he was already prepared."

There was a row of books, uniformly sized and bound, on the top of a small shelf, and I had the impression, possibly prompted in some since-forgotten way by Brooks, that those books were Montgomery Clift's personal collection of works by Freud. And I would eventually read Freud, though not for a while. Other writers, beginning with Kerouac, came first. Brooks never uttered the word "literature," but there's no question that that's what he meant when he shook his head and, a second later, breathed a gift that's enriched my life as no other, though I left his house empty-handed.

3301 WAVERLY DRIVE

JERRY AND MARY Neeley used to own the best video store on the east side of L.A. That's where I met them, and since they closed shop two years ago to sell movie collectibles online, we've occasionally met for coffee and talk of, among other topics, true crime. We've also kept in touch by e-mail, and last week Mary sent the following message:

> As you know the 40th anniversary of Tate/LaBianca is this August 8th & 9th. (Technically, the 9th & 10th because both parties were killed after midnight.)

> I wanted to go to the LaBianca house around 1 A.M. on the 10th to see if anyone else shows up. Would you be interested? I don't want to walk up there alone at 1 A.M.

Yes, I wrote back, I was interested. As her message indicates, she lives near the former residence of Rosemary and Leno LaBianca, who, around two in the morning on August 10, 1969, received a surprise visit from a hirsute, diminutive stranger—an erstwhile party guest at the house next door, and a convicted pimp with a harem of runaway girls, some of whom were waiting in a white and yellow '59 Ford parked at the curb.

Also in the Ford were a couple of boys who'd been drawn to the diminutive man in part because they, too, were serviced by his harem. They lived together, all of them, on a Western-town movie set on the outskirts of Los Angeles, where, under the influence of massive quantities of drugs, they were convinced that black militants aimed to destroy them, and the diminutive man, who called the shots, proposed to counterattack by perpetrating a series of gruesome murders and planting clues that would implicate the militants.

The diminutive man was Charles Manson, and the LaBiancas were fodder for his far-out blueprints. The previous night, others had been killed, though Manson wasn't present. Three of his retinue, including two who would participate in the LaBianca murders, invaded a house near Beverly Hills, where the actress Sharon Tate and four guests were hung, stabbed, shot, and bludgeoned. Tate was famously pregnant at the time, and her blood was used to paint the word PIG as a "clue" on the front door.

The Tate residence, at the crest of Cielo Drive, was designed to look like a French farmhouse. I went there a few times, though the house couldn't be seen without scaling the gate or the embankment that concealed it. I could just make out the edge of the garage, and once, from the top of a nearby hill, I got a good look at the roof, where workers were shingling, the reports of their hammers echoing across the canyon. I repeatedly dreamed of being inside the house. In my dreams, I'd often see the headlights of the killers as they drew closer and closer, and I'd rush about in a vain attempt to find and warn Tate and the others. *You can't change history*, I suppose those dreams were saying. *You can't save what's impossible to save.*

Nor could the house itself be saved. It was torn down at some point in the nineties, and a McMansion was raised in its place. The McMansion, as far as I know, has almost never been occupied, possibly due to super-stition or fear of lookie-loos – a legitimate fear, though people continue to visit. Last year, a friend from Providence flew to L.A. for the first time, and I asked if there was anything he especially wanted see. As a matter of fact, there was: the house on Cielo Drive. I drove him to where it used to be and pointed to the telephone pole climbed by one of the killers to snip the wires before the slaughter commenced.

I also drove my friend to the LaBianca house, which has been reno-vated since the terrible events of 1969. The front lawn has largely been paved, and a heavy gate stands between the house and the rest of Wa-verly Drive. According to Mary, who's something of a Manson-case expert, a visitor to the house, years after the murders, was shown the blood of the LaBiancas, which, though hidden by new carpeting, for-ever stained the floorboards.

I PICKED UP Mary on Sunday the 9th, just before midnight. Jerry, who suffers from diabetes, wasn't feeling well, so he couldn't come with us, but I'd invited two friends who live in the neighborhood to meet us on Wa-verly later. I circled the LaBianca house and, seeing no other lookie-loos, drove to a 7-Eleven, where Mary got a Coke and I got a coffee. Then, re-turning to Waverly, we parked as close as possible to the spot where Man-son had parked forty years before, and as soon as I cut the engine, we heard a heavy rattling sound and saw a man in silhouette chaining the gate in the LaBianca driveway. Was that something the occupants did ev-ery night, or were they especially wary due to the anniversary?

No matter; we sat in the car and talked, waiting for possible others. We were both struck by how quiet it was, and I was concerned about cops, since my car registration had lapsed, so we kept our voices low. Every so often a car would appear, but none slowed as they passed the house, where the occupants had retired, or so I assumed. All of the windows were dark, but at this moment forty years before, some of the windows would've been lit, since the LaBiancas had just returned home and Leno was reading the paper in the living room when Manson walked inside, possibly accompanied by his chief assassin, Tex Watson. (Accounts differ as to when Watson entered the house. Some say he helped Manson tie the LaBiancas, while others say Manson tied them alone and returned to the Ford, where Watson and the others were waiting to learn which of them would be selected to kill.) And what story was Leno reading in the paper? Conceivably the one about the Tate murders. Leno and his wife had bought the paper at a newsstand on their way home, and they had an exchange with the newsstand owner in which Mrs. LaBianca, in particular, expressed horror at the headline story. Now, an hour later, she and her husband were about to meet those responsible.

The friends I'd been expecting texted to say they weren't coming, and I noticed a small, dancing light maybe fifty yards away. I'd brought along binoculars, which Mary trained on the light. It was just a guy smoking, she said. We continued to talk, and she told me an anecdote I'd never heard: that when Manson walked inside the LaBianca living room (the door was unlocked), he saw a dog beside Leno on the couch and said, "Who you got with you? Sophia Loren?"

"I believe it," Mary said. "It sounds like something Manson would say."

It does for a fact. Manson had a sense of humor, unlike Hitler, whose ideology formed part of the basis of Manson's.

LIVING IN L.A., I've met several people who encountered Manson's victims and followers and others associated with the case.

My colleague Harry, for instance, had a brush with Sharon Tate when he was a teenager and dining in London with film director Nicholas Ray and Ray's son Tim, whom Harry had befriended at school. Ray, mean-time, was friendly with Roman Polanski, who stopped by their table to say hello, and with him was Sharon Tate, whom he would later marry but was then his girlfriend, as well as his co-star in *The Fearless Vampire Killers*, which he was also directing. At one point he and Ray broke off, leaving Tate alone with the boys, and though she sweetly did her best to engage them, her beauty rendered them mute.

The day before the massacre on Cielo Drive, my friend Burke's step-father, Joel, had his hair cut by Tate's former boyfriend, Jay Sebring, who was killed while trying to protect her. (Sebring was a noted men's hair stylist, responsible for Jim Morrison's lion mane; and indeed, on the day Joel had his hair cut at Sebring's salon, a celebrity was on hand: Jim Backus, who played Thurston Howell III on *Gilligan's Island*.)

Francis Schwartz, a wonderful man who practiced law well into his eighties, often observed Manson's girls outside the downtown court-house, where they daily held vigil during Manson's trial, shaving their heads and carving *X*s on their brows to attract attention.

My friend Michael once had lunch with Vincent Bugliosi, Manson's prosecutor and the co-author of *Helter Skelter*, the most celebrated ac-count of the case. Bugliosi was shocked when Michael told him he'd read *Helter Skelter* by way of lifting his mood, but he chuckled at Michael's explanation: he'd just been through a bad divorce, and he wanted to read about people who'd suffered worse.

And there are others, including Eve Babitz, a terrific writer whose books, save one, are inexplicably out of print. On separate occasions, Mary and I spoke to Babitz, who attended grammar school with the Manson girl known as Gypsy, and later became acquainted with Bobby Beausoleil, a Manson associate whose arrest for the murder of musician Gary Hinman sparked the Tate-LaBianca horrors.

"He was really beautiful," Babitz said of Beausoleil, "but he was such a downer. We used to call him Bummer Bob."

Beausoleil, incidentally, was briefly in the band Love, and he and Gypsy appeared in a Western-themed softcore flick that ends with a man being fatally knifed by Beausoleil.

Gary Hinman was fatally knifed by Beausoleil, after having his ear cut off by Manson.

Love, indeed.

BY 1:45, IT was starting to look like Mary and I were the only people curious enough to turn up at the LaBianca house. And maybe that was a good thing—I wasn't sure how I'd feel about somebody else doing what I was doing. It was morbid, but I preferred to think of it as harmless fun, like being in a movie about a stakeout at a haunted house—and if ever there were a house that deserved to be haunted, it's the one on Waverly Drive.

Headlights appeared at the far end of the street. They slowly got closer, and the car came into view. It was an eighties-model, white Cadillac, and I glanced through the rolled-up windows as it moved past my car, and saw four people—possibly teenagers—staring at the LaBianca house. A girl in the backseat kept her head low, as if wary of being seen. Then the Cadillac backed up and, halfway down the street, it began to move forward again, so obviously the occupants must be looking for the house number, which had been changed years before to hinder the curious. Watching the headlights incrementally advance, I flashed back to my dreams of Cielo Drive: the killers getting closer, impossible to stop. I wasn't scared, but I was spooked.

The Cadillac moved past us again, and I glanced at the girl in the backseat. She was wearing a hooded sweatshirt, with the hood now covering her head, which she continued to keep low. The Cadillac idled for a moment by the LaBianca gate before it moved down the hill and disappeared. Then I heard a door slam shut—or at least I thought I did. I asked Mary if she'd heard anything. We both listened to the deathly silence, and in my rearview mirror I saw a silhouette walk up the hill and toward the house.

"Somebody's coming!" I said.

"Shhhhhhh!" Mary said.

In fact, it was two people. I couldn't determine if they were male or female or one of each, but I could definitely make out two shapes. Then, for a split second, the house and the street close to it were filled with flashing light—the strobe of a camera, illuminating a girl who was standing in front of the gate. She wasn't the girl in the sweatshirt—or maybe it was her, but she'd left the sweatshirt in the Cadillac—and the person with the camera was a man. I got out of the car to exchange a few words or to possibly scare them in the spirit of fun, but they didn't seem to notice or care. They walked away in their own good time, two moving blobs in the darkness, and disappeared down the hill. I never heard them speak—not even a whisper along the lines of "Got the shot? Let's take another." Maybe they, too, were concerned about cops. Or maybe they thought *I* was a cop. But they managed to snap a picture of what had once been 3301 Waverly Drive at almost the precise minute when, forty years before, the unspeakable was occurring inside; and before I drove her home, Mary took a picture of her own.

THERE'S SOMETHING UNIQUELY L.A. about Manson: an aspiring rock star who lived on a movie set and, like an auteur, directed those eager to be molded. I think that partly accounts for my interest in him: he embodies something about the city that I've come to call home.

But there's more to it than that. In my novel, *Banned for Life*, the narrator speaks of visiting the Tate house, and, expressing sorrow that it was later destroyed, he adds, "In my view, considering the turning point it symbolized, it should have been preserved as a cultural landmark."

The narrator isn't me—not entirely—but I agree with him about the Tate house; and "the turning point" he mentions is the close of the sixties. My friend George once said that "the men who play golf" were deeply shaken by the sixties, and they took steps to make sure the decade wasn't repeated. George was vague about those steps, but I'm inclined to believe him, in part because it's obvious, to me at least, that Manson was used to frighten people already unsympathetic to youth culture. Some called him the most dangerous man alive. Really? Richard Nixon's body count exceeded Manson's by untold thousands. Nixon and his ilk were the true bogeymen, but Manson looked the part as they didn't—not to Joe Grabasandwich.

Meanwhile, there's only one other true-crime case that intrigues me as much as the Manson case: the JFK assassination. For a long time, I saw no connection. I was interested in the JFK case largely because of the enigma of Lee Harvey Oswald: did he do it or didn't he? I was inclined to think he did—alone, in fact. Then I had an exchange with my friend Demetri, who said, "Well, if Oswald did it, you could say he started the sixties, just as Manson ended them."

So there *was* a connection. It explained a great deal.

But not everything. I think, finally, it goes back to Sharon Tate. But for her, I don't know that I would ever have thought much about Manson. She's the reason I dreamed about the house on Cielo Drive. As a child, I thought Tate was the most beautiful woman who'd ever lived. And that leads to another quote from my friend George. We were talking about Greek mythology one night, and he said, "You know, I don't

think any of those stories are relevant anymore. I mean, killing your father and fucking your mother and plucking out your eyes—that's a perfect myth for two thousand years ago. But a beautiful blonde movie star
being murdered at her mansion in the Hollywood Hills—*there's* a myth
for *our* time."

And so in that way she stands, along with the house that used to be
3301 Waverly Drive.

NORMAN MAILER AND THE SHAPE OF MY NOSE

BACK WHEN I was a cool kid living in New York, I was friendly with a character actor named Sully Boyar. Sully appeared in numerous movies, among them *Fort Apache the Bronx*, with Paul Newman; *The Jazz Singer*, with Neil Diamond; *In the Soup*, with Steve Buscemi; and *Car Wash*, with Richard Pryor. The last movie on that list was 1970s Afro-cinema, and Sully played the car-wash owner, so that sometimes, when he was walking around Manhattan, black guys would come up and say, "Didn't I used to work for your ass?" They were sure they had.

Sully had known Al Pacino since Pacino was a teenager and Sully was a judge about to step down from the bench to pursue acting, and they shared the screen in *Serpico*, *The Panic in Needle Park*, and *Dog Day After-noon*. I'd long wanted to meet Pacino, and when Sully asked me to tend bar at his daughter's wedding reception, I figured I might get the chance. It was an outdoor reception with a great many Italian guests (Sully's wife, Jo, was Sicilian), and at one point, as I poured champagne, a cry went up and I saw a swarm of Italian ladies rushing to pinch the cheeks of, yes, Al Pacino, who'd just arrived. He was dressed like a hippie, like his charac-ter in *Serpico*, in a flak jacket and a yellow headband, and he had a dog with him—a dog, I remember, fittingly named Lucky, having been adopted at the pound. Then Sully saved Pacino from the Italian ladies and escorted him to the bar. I think he had a Sprite. Whatever it was, I know it was alcohol-free.

I had a second brush with Pacino three years later at the Actors Studio. Sully, a Studio member, had arranged for me to observe sessions, and every Friday morning I'd take the subway from Williamsburg to the Studio in Hell's Kitchen, where Sully would praise me as an actor of promise to influential members. He'd vaguely praised me to Pacino three years before, and now, outside the Studio, he did it again. Pacino extended his hand. I wrenched it. I was nervous – as nervous as I'd been at the wedding reception – and I finally returned his hand, which he flapped as if shaking off pain, and said, in his very best Al Pacino voice, "Wow! This guy is powerful!"

"Yeah," Sully said. "He's a sheepherder."

I was not, and never have been, a sheepherder. My father kept sheep on his farm in Virginia, but no herding was involved; I simply fed them and helped my father shear them. Oh, and I also had to walk out to their goddamned shed in the middle of the freezing night during lambing season to see if any lambs had been born. I hate sheep. (I was about to write "I hate fucking sheep," but that would read as if I've fucked sheep, which I'm sure I would've hated doing if I had.)

So I was kind of mad at Sully for telling Al Pacino I was a sheepherder. Still, like me, he was nervous around Pacino, whose celebrity had come between them, and Sully was chronically unemployed – the actor's curse – and hoping Pacino would throw him a job. He never did, as far as I know, and that goes for Sully's other celebrity friends. He was constantly talking about his sorry financial state – and when Sully talked, it was hard to shut him up. He was, by his own admission, a babbler, and many people, I'm sure, avoided him for that reason.

One night I had dinner with Sully, who surprised me with an extra ticket for a play about Marilyn Monroe. The play, *Strawhead*, was being workshopped for two nights only at the Studio, and it was written and directed by Norman Mailer, one of my favorite writers.

Now, Mailer has often been criticized for his gassy prolixity, but his detractors are usually unacquainted with his best stuff, or so I've found. *The Executioner's Song* is, I think, a masterpiece. So is Mailer's book about the Apollo 11 mission, *Of a Fire on the Moon*, and his political journalism is peerless. This is from a profile of the Kennedys, written in 1960 after Mailer had spent some time with Jackie Kennedy, who famously detested politics:

> "Do you think she's happy?" asked a lady, an old friend, on the beach at Wellfleet.
> "I guess she would rather spend her life on the Riviera."
> "What would she do there?"
> "End up as the mystery woman, maybe, in a good murder case."

In fact, after JFK was gunned down in 1963 – easily the most discussed murder case of the late twentieth century – Jackie was always viewed as something of a mystery, since she never spoke publicly about that awful day. Later, she married the shipping tycoon Aristotle Onassis, and did indeed spend much time on yachts in the Mediterranean, thus ratifying Mailer's impression. The man was brilliant. Some of his descriptions of real-life people point almost to X-ray vision, so much was he able to extrapolate from details typically overlooked. Even the shape of a nose could reveal occult character to Mailer. He was a prodigious face reader.

So, part of me never wanted to meet Mailer, afraid of what he might conclude from the shape of my nose. But I did want to see his play, so I walked with Sully to the Studio, which was packed. The seats in the upstairs theater were arranged in a C-shape around the stage, and Mailer's seat faced mine, while Sully sat a few rows below me. Then the lights dimmed and Mailer's daughter, Kate, took the stage. She was playing Marilyn Monroe. That was strange. Mailer had publicly lusted after Monroe, and he'd cast his daughter in the part. He'd also cast his wife, Norris Church, as Monroe's friend Amy Greene, and at one point Norris and Kate performed a quasi-erotic dance, and I looked across the room at Mailer. It was dark, of course, but I noticed his hands, which were folded over his belly, rise and fall as he breathed heavily. My God, he was breathing heavily as he watched his daughter, playing a woman he wanted to fuck, do an erotic dance with her stepmother. Things were getting stranger and stranger.

In fact, the play proved tame. Still, I thought it was a terrific play, as good as I'd hoped, and I couldn't get over how privileged I was to be seeing it. I walked down to Sully during the intermission to say as much, and he said, "Oh, it's a *terrible* play. It's the *worst*."

On and on he went, explaining why it was such a bad play. I've forgotten his reasons, but I respected him enormously and decided he must be right. Then I realized that everyone, except for me, was seated again and I was delaying the start of the second act. And Norman Mailer was staring at me. Yes, I was now the subject of his X-ray vision, and who knew what was going through his mind about this oblivious kid, hipster-haired and leather-jacketed, who was causing him and everyone else to wait. I somehow managed to extricate myself from Sully, who was still babbling, and hurried to my seat and, even after the lights dimmed, saw that Mailer was staring at me. Was he angry? Was he reading my character, faults and all, from the shape of my nose? I could no longer enjoy the play. Not that I would've enjoyed it even if Mailer *hadn't* just read my character from the shape of my nose. No, Sully had convinced me the play was bad, and bad it was. I could hardly wait for it to finish.

Then it did, and I walked down to Sully, who said, "You know, the second act wasn't bad at all."

Wow, thanks. You ruined the play for me, and now you decide you like it. Meanwhile, Mailer was standing by the only public exit in the theater and thanking every member of the audience for turning out. Now I was going to have to meet Mailer, who'd have a close-up view of my nose. I dawdled, hoping he'd leave before I did; and when no one remained but the two of us, I stepped forward and, nervously offering my hand, said, "I'm a huge fan."

Well, if you know anything about Mailer, you know he appointed himself Hemingway's heir in the macho-writer department. He brawled. He debated feminists. He stabbed one of his six wives. And yet, as I stood there shaking his hand, I took him in, three feet away, and realized he was shy at heart. I could tell, as one animal sizing up another, just as I could tell that he was taken aback at my compliment. Maybe he didn't expect it from someone so young, or maybe it owed to my nervous sincerity, which contrasted with the way I was dressed. Then, as if to correct the glitch in his disguise, he thrust out his chest and said in a voice unnaturally deep, "Thank you."

Those were the only two words he said to me, and if I had to pick just two, they'd be nice ones to have. And I have them still. Everywhere I go, they go with me.

Meanwhile, there are books full of words he didn't say to me personally, and they survive, while Mailer himself is dead. And Sully is dead, too, though he survives on film, speaking the words of others to, among others, Al Pacino.

HIGHWAY 46 REVISITED

I NEVER THOUGHT I looked like James Dean, as people used to say I did, especially after I moved to New York. We shared the same coloring, but I was tall and lanky, while he was short and muscular. My face was round, and his was rectangular. Moreover, I strove as an actor to be as natural as possible, and Dean's acting struck me as excessive, which is now what I most enjoy about it. His excess wasn't of the soap-opera sort; it was quirkily personal, as when he rolls a cold bottle of milk over his brow to calm himself in *Rebel Without a Cause*. His character in *Rebel* is lacking the love—that is, milk—of his shrewish mother, and the symbolic way it's expressed is one of many Kabuki-like gestures in Dean's performances, particularly in scenes involving parents. His biography speaks to the reason. His mother died when he was nine, and afterward his father sent him to live on a relative's farm in faraway Indiana.

Prior to discovering Dean, I was embarrassed by having come from a farming family. That was déclassé where I grew up, but if James Dean had been a farm boy, maybe it was okay for me to be one. Meanwhile, even though I wasn't impressed with Dean's acting, I was pleased to be told I resembled him, since he was a classic movie star, with the kind of arty pedigree I craved for myself.

And so, to coax further comparisons, I entered my James Dean phase. I slouched like Dean, and mumbled like Dean, and had my hair cut like his. I aped his expressions, and chewed the tip of my shirt collar, which Dean used to do, or so I'd learned. I also learned where he used to live—a garret on West 68th Street—and a couple of times I stood outside, staring at the windows, as if that could cause him to appear and provide pointers on how to better imitate him: "Okay, when you're doing that thing with your eyebrows? Try to look hurt, not angry. Like this." Bear in mind that I was still in my teens; and I personally knew a number of actors similarly obsessed with Dean. One of them was a roommate, and he relocated soon after his sort-of-girlfriend announced that I looked more like Dean than he did.

Dean continues to influence actors, though those now in their twenties, disinterested in history, may not realize how much they owe him. His idiosyncratic approach to acting has never been replicated (despite, in some cases, considerable effort); it's his image—the misunderstood, beautiful, sensitive yet dangerous loner—that goes on being recycled, as per Robert Pattinson, of the *Twilight* movies, and James Franco, who played Dean in a made-for-TV biopic. Dean was acutely aware of his image; he cultivated relationships with photographers who documented his every mood and move, and some of the results, such as Dennis Stock's shot of Dean walking in a Times Square downpour, are familiar to people who've never seen *Rebel Without a Cause*, *East of Eden*, or *Giant*. Even Dean's final moments, on September 30, 1955, were caught on film. He was on his way from Los Angeles to a car race in Salinas, California (the setting of *East of Eden*), in a silver Porsche Spyder, and following in a second car, at Dean's request, was photographer Sanford Roth. Dean wasn't well acquainted with the Spyder, which he'd recently purchased, and the drive to Salinas was intended to prepare him for the race. He was ticketed for speeding near Bakersfield, shortly before he stopped for a Coke at a gas station called Blackwell's Corner on Highway 466 (now 46). At the same time, Donald Turnupseed, a California Polytechnic Institute student, was making his way home from school. He struck the Spyder, which he couldn't see due to the slant of the sun, as he was making a left turn onto Highway 41. Dean, whose neck was broken, was photographed by Roth as he was being lifted into an ambulance, dying or already dead at the age of twenty-four.

MY JAMES DEAN phase didn't last long. I developed my own style as an actor, and if I passed one of Dean's movies while channel surfing, I might stop and watch, but I rarely thought of him otherwise, especially after I moved to L.A., where I focused more on writing than acting. Every so often, if someone asked me, I'd do a part in a movie. I appeared in a number of experimental shorts directed by my friend Burke, once alongside our mutual friend Paul, who reminded me a little of James Dean. It wasn't because of his looks. He had his Swedish mother's features and his Filipino father's dark hair and complexion, so that he was often taken for Latin. Still, his soulful intensity evoked Dean, if only, again, a little, and he was one of the best actors I knew, in spite of – or maybe, in part, because of – his indifference to acting. Like so many people, he *really* wanted to direct, and he was frustrated with his lack of progress in that way, and frustrated with his life in general. He had family problems – a religious upbringing, a disapproving stepfather, and so on – and he meantime felt he was being used by friends who sought his help with filmmaking projects of their own. There's a lot of that kind of thing in L.A. – "Can you come down to the set and PA for a couple of days?" – and good-natured Paul invariably said yes, while resenting himself for saying yes, just as he resented those who asked for his help in the first place. It was a recurring theme in our conversations. He was giving all his time to others, which meant his own work wasn't getting done, and he was almost thirty, with nothing to show for himself.

Paul's friend Jake was another actor with directing ambitions, and Paul had naturally agreed to help on a short film that Jake was planning to shoot in his hometown, Santa Cruz. Meanwhile, Jake asked if I'd act in the film. I told him yes, as long as I didn't have to drive to Santa Cruz, suggesting that I ride with Paul.

Then Paul backed out. Then he agreed to help again. Then he backed out again. And so on. I felt bad for Jake, who was a good guy in his own right, and one night I phoned Paul to press him for a final decision. He *couldn't* go to Santa Cruz, he said; his car wouldn't survive the drive.

"Well, you can ride with Jake," I said. "I mean, you told him you were going to help, right? I think you're kind of obligated."

In all the time I'd known Paul, I'd never heard him raise his voice. Now I did.

"All right!" he snapped. "I'll do it!" He was oddly subdued after that. He sounded half asleep when he spoke at all, as if sapped by his brief outburst.

Jake was driving to Santa Cruz a day ahead of the cast, and Paul was now going with him, so Jake arranged for me to ride with an actor named Howard, who knocked on my door an hour late. He was Chinese and sixty-five, at least, and holding a huge soft drink he'd stopped to buy on the way, being fond of junk food, as I was about to learn. I got into his car and had a look at the directions Jake had sent him. We would be taking Interstate 5 to Highway 46 to reach the 101; and as a touch of local color, Jake had noted the James Dean death site on the 46, as well as Blackwell's Corner, where Dean stopped before the crash.

Like Paul, I'd had reservations about going to Santa Cruz. I was very busy and couldn't spare the time to work on a film for free. Still, once I saw Jake's directions, I was eager to hit the road. I thought of the trip as a gift to myself as a kid, when I was at the peak of my James Dean phase. That kid would've loved to have seen the place where Dean died, and now, through older eyes, he would.

HOWARD WAS ORIGINALLY from San Francisco, he told me, and he worked for a long time in finance in New York, turning to acting late in life. We naturally talked about New York, as well as acting, while zooming past orange groves and fields full of sun-scorched weeds. We also stopped repeatedly for fast food, which Howard unwrapped and ate as he drove, sometimes removing both hands from the wheel, chomping loudly and looking out the window, looking everywhere, it seemed, except at the road. Wouldn't it be funny if I got killed near the spot where James Dean died? In fact, it wouldn't be. But the closer we got to that spot, the more I thought about the possibility of crashing, so that the next time Howard removed his hands from the wheel to snack, meanwhile doing eighty and staring at the scenery as the car edged toward the road's shoulder, I said, "Howard, look out!"

"What?"

"You're going off the road!"

Of course he now looked at me, not the road. Then he looked at the road and set the car right. Then he unwrapped another snack, taking his hands off the wheel, staring at the snack instead of the road, again while doing eighty.

"Howard, look out!"

"What?"

Jake called to ask about our progress. I felt like saying he was soon to be short two actors and he might want to think about recasting. Instead, I asked about the James Dean death site at the juncture of the 46 and the 41: was it easy to miss? It wasn't, he said, and neither was Blackwell's Corner, which had a huge picture of Dean outside of it.

Howard was almost as interested in seeing the crash site as I was. Dean was "family," he said, meaning he was a fellow actor. We watched for Blackwell's Corner. We didn't see it. We also watched for signs announcing the 41. There were such signs, but then we were in wine country, with vineyards everywhere and signs foretelling the approach of Paso Robles. I had another look at Jake's directions. If we were near Paso Robles, we'd long since passed the 41.

"Goddamn it!" I said. "We missed it!"

I wanted to turn around, but we'd gotten a late start, since Howard had stopped for fast food on his way to my place, and we'd also lost time due to our frequent stops for still more fast food. Howard said we could see the James Dean death site on the trip back. Then, spotting a Subway in Paso Robles, he stopped, and we went inside and ate – again.

IT TURNED OUT that Paul had driven his own car to Santa Cruz, even though he'd said it wouldn't survive the trip. I, meanwhile, was unconvinced I'd survive another trip with Howard, so I asked Paul if I could hitch a ride with him after the shoot. Of course, he said, acting strangely. Jake likewise noticed that Paul was acting strangely. I didn't know what he was supposed to be doing on the set, but I never saw him do anything except stand, with a vacant expression, beside the camera crew. At times, between takes, he and I would talk in the parking lot of the motel where we slept and worked (the motel, two blocks from the ocean, was the setting of the movie), and he appeared relatively lively. Then, the break over, he would stand again on the set, doing nothing with a vacant expression.

The day of departure came. I hated to leave Santa Cruz. I'd woken early every morning and walked to the pier, where I'd watched sunbathing sea lions loudly quarrel. Then, backtracking, I'd lingered at the Spanish-style apartment complex where I pictured myself living. I could write such beautiful words there, I thought. I could be so happy.

I was insane, of course. I consider myself, more or less, politically progressive, but I could never be progressive enough for Santa Cruz. After a few weeks, people would storm my place with torches, like villagers in Frankenstein movies of yore. I returned from my final walk on the pier to the motel, where Paul was in the parking lot, zoned out as ever. What was wrong with him? He didn't know, he told me. He hadn't slept in days. He felt like he had a brain disorder. It sounded like he was depressed, I said; we could talk about it on the drive. He knew I wanted to see the James Dean death site; and since he, too, had missed it on the drive from L.A., together we'd seek the juncture of the 46 and the 41.

WE PASSED ARTICHOKE fields and stopped for tacos near a town that bills itself as the artichoke capitol of the world. Paul seemed more himself again, and we discussed movies, our families, the people we knew in common—all our usual subjects—as wine country unfurled around us. There were fewer and fewer vineyards on the 46, and almost none by the time we saw signs announcing the 41—but which badly marked turnoff *was* the 41? Finally, convinced we'd just passed it, I asked Paul to go back. He did. The turnoff road was thin, with a fountain on one side of the entrance. A lush tree shaded the fountain, which advertised a winery, and the bleak fields in the distance were checkered with tiny houses. Nothing about this place recalled photos I'd seen of the crash.

Still, we parked and got out. Paul lay in the carpet grass beneath the
tree, apparently napping, while I walked to the stop sign at the intersection of the 46 and the turnoff road, which I now suspected was not the
41. A car slowed and paused at the stop sign, a middle-aged couple inside
the car. They were locals, I could tell, and I approached them and said,
"Yeah, I'm looking for the place James Dean died?"

"Do you know his address?" one of them asked. "Hell," I wanted
to say. Hadn't they heard the word "died"? Hadn't they heard of James
Dean? He was bound to figure prominently in regional lore.

I was too disgusted to ask again. The couple drove off, and I sat for
a while by the fountain. The sound of trickling water was peaceful, off-
setting the sounds of occasional traffic. Eventually, Paul rose from the
shaded grass and we continued on the 46, and five or ten minutes later,
I saw a big green sign that read: JAMES DEAN MEMORIAL JUNCTION.
Yes, here at last was the 41, looking exactly as it had in the photos I'd
seen – how could I have missed it on the drive with Howard?

Paul pulled over, and I got out to snap a picture. I could easily envi-
sion the crash. I watched cars speed down the hill on the 46 where Dean
had seen Donald Turnupseed's car, about to make a left onto the 41, and
said, "That guy's gotta stop," to his German mechanic, Rolf Wütherich,
who was accompanying Dean to Salinas, and who was later killed in another car crash. Wütherich barely survived the crash with Dean. He was
hospitalized for months, and his injuries, compounded by the hate mail
he received from Dean's fans, led to psychiatric problems that afflicted
him for the rest of his life.

Paul and I drove on. We stopped at Blackwell's Corner where there
was for a fact a huge picture of James Dean outside it: a color picture of
his head and shoulders. Inside, posters and postcards of Dean were for
sale, and the only two people present, aside from me and Paul, were bored
teenaged staffers. They, I knew, were locals who'd heard of James Dean.

Paul dropped me at my apartment at dusk. The whites of his eyes were alarmingly red, but he was in a good mood: I remember him laughing just before he drove off. Our adventure had made us better friends, I thought. He would go home and sleep. His depression would lift. He would embrace his stellar acting talent, as I would certainly encourage him to do.

I never got the chance. I saw him only once – briefly – after we returned from Santa Cruz. He broke contact with me and almost every friend he had, and his former roommate eventually sent me a message about him. Paul was now living with his mother, the message said, and when he abruptly left his old place, he left most of his belongings behind. The message didn't say if Paul was now happy; it only said that he was a completely different person from the person he used to be.

We all used to be different people: an actor with designs on directing; an actor who styled himself after James Dean; an actor who really was James Dean and became, in a flash, a memory.

PRINCE HOLDEN

After J.D. Salinger's death in January 2010, contributors to The Nervous Breakdown, including D.R. Haney, paid collective tribute by writing short pieces about Salinger.

WHEN I WAS a sophomore in high school, a girl named Dena, amused by some standard-issue angry-young-man barb of mine, said, "My God, you're just like *Holden*." The girls by her side nodded in agreement, but I didn't know who Holden was. It wasn't until a few years later, after I'd moved to the Lower East Side of Manhattan, that I read *The Catcher in the Rye* and understood Dena's comparison. Of course, I was only one of the hordes of disaffected youth who identified with Holden Caulfield, but I considered myself a special case, in part because I was living a post-punk version of *Catcher* on Holden's home turf.

In fact, I wasn't. Salinger was an uptown writer, and Holden was a maladjusted preppie who passed no sparks with the subculture types who flourished downtown, as they had for at least a century prior to the appearance of *Catcher*. I was closer in spirit to the Village-based Beats, I decided, especially Kerouac; and Holden's fractiousness, compared to mine, seemed tepid on second thought, concluding as it did in therapy. Like

Shakespeare's Prince Hal, Holden was a dilettantish rebel, unwilling or unable to break free of a Brahmin family.

So my analysis used to run. Now I see just how much Salinger and the Beats had in common, with their shared interest in Eastern mysticism, and their mutual anticipation of 1960s youth culture, which has influenced the world ever since. And in recent years, the culture has taken another turn – or am I the only person to notice that Salinger's death coincided with the introduction of the iPad? Will *The Catcher in the Rye* continue to thrive? One hopes. There are more imperiled kids to catch than ever.

(Top) A bank job in *Daddy's Boys*, the Roger Corman production that led me to abandon New York for L.A. *(Bottom)* Shooting *Daddy's Boys* at Newhall movie ranch, once owned by silent-era star William S. Hart. The titular Daddy, Raymond J. Barry, is beside me at right.

(Top) Pensive between takes on *Drugi Čovek*, the first of two movies I made in Belgrade. *(Bottom)* Shooting *Drugi Čovek* outside Hotel Metropol, where I lived during production. I was very unhappy on that movie; my next in Belgrade was a different story, so much so that I hated to leave.

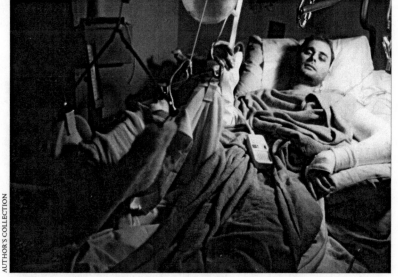

(Top) A small party on the set of *Life Among the Cannibals* for actress Juliet Landau, who's between me and director Harry Bromley-Davenport. *(Bottom)* High on morphine at Cedars-Sinai Hospital shortly after I was struck by a car in a Hollywood crosswalk. Months of physical therapy and reconstructive surgery followed.

MARY NEELEY

SARA MATTHEWS

(Above) The former LaBianca residence on the fortieth anniversary of the Manson murders. The small circle at left has been identified by a metaphysical type as a "ghost orb." *(Right)* Outside the White House in my early teens, with my sister, Dawn, and my brother, David, whose testimony would one day solve the mystery of the missing Farrah Fawcett dollar.

(Above) Stoned at a gathering in my first apartment in Belgrade. My friend Miloš, at left, holds a drumstick signed by Jason Reece of …And You Will Know Us by the Trail of Dead, which I'd brought from the U.S. for luck. *(Left)* At work on *Banned for Life* in Montenegro during a weekend retreat from Belgrade.

A sample of the photos of *Banned for Life* that were sent by friends, who correctly judged a first-time novelist's vanity. *(Left)* TJ Nordaker kisses a *Banned* spine. *(Below)* Jeremy Lowe departs for Asia. *(Opposite page, clockwise from top left)* John T. Woods gives great face; Kymberlee della Luce betters John; *Banned* at the center of Connie Money's vintage record collection; Zara Potts' *Banned* breakfast in Auckland, New Zealand; Rimbaud Brandenstein, a *Banned* reader of the future.

JOHN T. WOODS

KYMBERLEE DELLA LUCE

CONNIE MONEY

COREY BRANDENSTEIN

ZARA POTTS

(Above) Trying hard as a teenager to channel *The Wild One* in a peacoat. Black leather jackets were scarce in Virginia. *(Right)* At the height of my James Dean phase. The imitation improves frame by frame.

V. LIBER

AND A NEW CHAPTER BEGINS

I SPENT NINE years writing *Banned for Life*. I consider that a long time to work on a book. James Joyce, whose name I'm unfit to mention by way of comparison, worked on *Ulysses* for eight years, and that book is longer than mine by more than three hundred pages. (I write these words on Bloomsday.)

Was it worth it? I don't know, yet. It will depend, I suppose, on how the book is received. At the moment, a number of friends are reading *Banned*, but, with a few exceptions, those who've finished haven't told me they've finished, maybe because they didn't like the book and don't want to hurt my feelings, or because they did like it and aren't sure how to express it. I'm an Author now. It's not a big deal to me at all, being an Author, but some of my friends might regard it as a big deal, since so many people have vague plans to one day write a book but deep down suspect they'll never get around to it. A couple of friends have announced their jealousy, or as one of them, a comely Scot, put it: "I'd like to slap your face!"

"Hey," I told her, "if you want to spend nine years of daily torture working on a book, go for it."

Of course, there was a compliment in what she said, and I've lately had compliments in the form of photos, one from my friend Jeremy Lowe. He bought a copy of *Banned* just before he left for a long trek around Asia, and he posed with the book at LAX. That was a month ago, and I didn't know about his photo till he wrote me from Thailand to say that he'd read and loved *Banned*, adding that I should search his Facebook wall for something labeled "Ousted from L.A." I was blown away. I had no idea that my book would, or could, mean enough to him that he'd take such a picture. He left his copy of *Banned* behind at a Thai hostel, where, he wrote me, he hoped that someone else would find and read it—another gesture that blew me away.

And then there was the photo my friend TJ Nordaker sent me on MySpace, in which he's kissing his copy of *Banned*. TJ's caption read: *I don't have any fucking words, so I took this picture.* I called to thank him, and he asked me a number of questions about *Banned*. Did I really do such and such? Was there really such a person as X? I hated to disappoint with some of my answers. I've led an eventful life, which I daresay has been as eventful as the life of the *Banned* narrator, but my book is a novel and not a memoir. Besides, as Norman Mailer, among others, has said, all writing is fiction. We discard, as we tell stories, certain details and emphasize others, sometimes because of faulty memory, and sometimes because the alterations simply make for a better story.

Meanwhile, it seems to me that the story behind the writing of a book—any book—is easily as interesting as the story told in the book itself. Nine years certainly provided me with abundant material. I spent the last four months of 2007 and the spring and early summer of 2008, for instance, building and winning a court case against my landlords, who were trying to evict me. I lived in Belgrade, Serbia, with a few gaps, from 2000 to 2002, where I indulged my fondness for controlled substances, and frequently visited other Eastern European capitals, including Warsaw and Budapest. I almost started a band with friends in L.A. in 2006, but they started it without me before I attended a single practice, thus breaking my heart, which was also broken – repeatedly – by a girl on whom a significant character in *Banned* is based. I was devastated by the 2004 reelection of George W. Bush, unable to move for two days, which I spent on my sofa with a blanket covering my head; and I napped on Election Day 2008, woken by the sound of cheering in the street and so knew that Barack Obama had won. I supported myself almost exclusively through writing, completing a number of commissioned screenplays and contributing pieces to zines and alt-weeklies, and had a poem translated into Icelandic and published in a book in (where else?) Iceland. I acted in movies, including Harry Bromley-Davenport's *Frozen Kiss*, which I wrote under an assumed name, and Jennifer Lynch's *Surveillance*, which I shot in Saskatchewan, and occasionally supplemented my income as an art-department assistant on movies, a courier, an air-purifier salesman, and a pizza maker/delivery guy. There were a number of deaths to be endured: Kerry, my on-off girlfriend of several years; my angelic grandmother, Cornelia; a feral cat named Roro who'd elected to live with me; and a dog named Roxy who used to camp outside my apartment in the hope that, if and when I drove to the store, I'd let her ride along. (She loved riding in cars, that dog, and she ended up getting killed by one, when she was rattled by exploding fireworks on the Fourth of July and dashed into the street – something she ordinarily would never have done.) I fell out with a few old friends and made new ones, including TJ and the Die Princess Die crew. Two of my three brothers got married, and I flew to Virginia for the weddings, just as I always tried to visit my family in Virginia every Christmas and, if possible, stop in New York to visit friends who are like family, I've known them so long. Out-of-town guests came and went: John and Sabine from New York, Jon from Providence, and Bill from Portland, whose great band, Federation X, crashed at my place while touring. I met with potential publishers, including one from Portland, and flew up to discuss details, crashing with Bill, and shook hands on a deal that fell through shortly afterward, when a friend of the publisher read the *Banned* manuscript and declared it politically unacceptable. I acquired two new nephews, brothers of my first. I went to countless shows and wrote songs that will probably never be heard by anybody. I did readings, including one I somehow survived, despite a bottle of Cutty Sark. I drank too much in general, and had panic attacks that almost sent me to the hospital, meanwhile suffering from testicular pain that I was sure must be due to cancer, though tests revealed it wasn't. I frequently got sick, always a favorite host of the common cold virus, and I broke a finger after tripping on a wire across the street from the Silver Lake music venue Spaceland, and successfully sued with the help of a lawyer whose office was lined with photos of himself surfing. I had a car impounded by the city, two others die, and I'm presently trying to kill the fourth car I've owned since the turn of the century. I was interviewed—or supposed to be interviewed—on L.A.'s Indie 103.1, but I could barely speak, between my loquacious friend Burke, who appeared on the show with me, and the Suicide Girls, whose show it was and is. I met a number of admired figures, including Elliott Smith, Thurston Moore, and Mark Ames, whose Moscow-based alt-weekly *The eXile* inspired me to journey to Eastern Europe, and who later quoted me in a piece for *The eXile*: a joke I'd made about human-raping, wife-beating dolphins. And through every bit of it (and this list is obviously far from complete) I worked on *Banned for Life*. For nine fucking years. And then one day the first copy arrived, and a friend said, "Wow, you must be stoked, huh?"

"I guess. But, you know, it looks so small, compared to what I was expecting."

"*Small?* It's four hundred pages long!"

"I know. But after working on it for nine years, it feels like it should be the size of the Manhattan Yellow Pages."

Still, it was here. Yes, it had finally come: a decade, very nearly, that could be held and even kissed by friends, including those I have yet to make.

THE VIRGIN INTERVIEW: A DISCUSSION ABOUT *BANNED FOR LIFE* WITH MEGAN POWER

One of the original contributors to The Nervous Breakdown, Megan Power is currently in a postgraduate creative writing program at Trinity University in Carmarthen, Wales. Her interview with D.R. Haney, conducted by e-mail, appeared at TNB in July 2009.

"IT ALL BEGAN with a fuck" goes the brash opening line of D.R. Haney's first novel, *Banned for Life*, and the strange seduction begins.

For those who haven't read Haney's sprawling debut, it follows Jason Maddox's seriocomic adventures in the underground punk scene, stretching beyond mosh-pit mayhem and barroom brawls to explore death and obsession and purpose. The author zigzags confidently between a resonant coming-of-age tale in North Carolina, *la vie bohéme* in hardscrabble New York, and a tempestuous L.A. love affair that leads our narrator to Belgrade for climax and denouement.

Even readers ambivalent to punk will be drawn in by the peculiarly irresistible voice of Jason, who is at turns heartthrob, heartbroken, and healed.

D.R. Haney tells The Nervous Breakdown how he went from breaking guitars to becoming a serious novelist.

You've said it took nine years to write the four-hundred-page book. What prevented you from going permanently insane during that time?
I'm not sure I didn't. It was quite a ride. I mean, if there's no blood on the keyboard, there should be. Broken bone and gray matter, too.

I was lucky to have good friends. That was my saving grace – that and music. It's perhaps an embarrassing thing to say, but rock & roll has been a redemptive factor throughout my life. If I'm feeling bad, I only have to pick up a guitar or play a certain record, like "Arboretum" by Unwound or "The Rat" by the Walkmen, and my mood improves. My spiritual sense is absolutely tied to music, and specifically to rock & roll.

Jason, the protagonist and narrator, confesses late in the book that his story is memoir "written as a novel for legal reasons." Can you talk about this?
Well, the book certainly isn't a memoir, but if it were, Jason would no doubt be worried about the potential for legal fallout, and just plain fallout, period.

I'll say this much: there are characters in *Banned* who are very much based on real-life people, and I was (and continue to be) concerned with their reactions. I didn't even bother to change the names in a few cases. Others are composites or purely the product of my imagination. But I think all narrative writing is finally fiction; it's only a matter of degree.

Morally, Banned *seems concerned with the search for personal meaning, which is achieved, mainly, through defeating a particularly American brand of boredom. Would you agree with this assessment?*
To a certain extent, yes, though I think the American brand is something we've successfully exported to the rest of the world through movies and TV shows. American entertainment is hugely popular, even among those

who claim to hate us, and its appeal is its mindlessness, in never allowing the viewer to become bored, when in fact boredom is the very thing it produces, no matter the initial giddiness.

For me, it's worse than mere boredom; it amounts to the starvation of the soul, in dimmed senses, in unwitting complacency and conformity and alienation. It's a culture of death. Ironically, death in America is a subject largely avoided, which to me is classically Freudian: you don't want mentioned what you suspect yourself, perhaps rightly, to be.

I'm not proposing this as an original view. It's been argued again and again, and there are counterarguments, but when the subject comes up in conversation, I've almost never had anyone disagree with me. Most of us seem to recognize the effects of what I'm calling the culture of death, if not in ourselves then others. But there's also a general feeling of, well, what's to be done about it? That's the world we live in. And it is. But the question for me at that point is: how to stay alive?

There's obviously no single answer, but I do think, as you say, Jason in *Banned* is searching for a way that will work for him, and a classic starting point for anyone alienated of Jason's generation was punk rock because it was forthrightly expressing rage in a way that was forbidden, and continues to be, by mainstream media. These were kids who, whatever their flaws, refused to go along with the program, and that's something I don't really see anymore. I don't think there will be another movement like punk in my lifetime, because we're all too atomized and prematurely (in the case of the young) jaded, but I want to leave a record of what was, and I think and hope *Banned* can be appreciated by people who dislike punk but nevertheless have a streak of resistance in them, or they're looking to discover or recover it. That's what happened to Jason: he both discovered and had to recover it, having once again succumbed to the culture of death.

I couldn't get past hating the character of Irina. She's insecure, a compulsive liar, intellectually unimpressive, and yet Jason fetishizes her physical beauty. Did you intend for her to be so unlikable?

It's interesting; I've had a number of women readers react as you did, but almost never any male readers. I don't know if that's because men are more superficial than women, if they're more easily bamboozled by physical beauty or what, but even male musicians I know—guys with deep roots in the punk scene—will read the book and comment mostly on Irina, and rarely in unfavorable terms. And, you know, in the book, Irina says that women don't like her, so it seems as though that trend carries over with readers.

But to answer your question: I certainly wanted the reader to be exasperated by Irina, to feel about her as Jason feels as she leads him on this agonizing ride of *l'amour fou*. The reader is sort of Jason's confidante, and if a friend comes to you and says, "And then she did *this*," you're almost certainly going to take his side. But I personally believe Irina when she says she's forced to lie because Jason is too possessive to listen when she tries to tell him the truth.

As for her physical beauty, that's another funny thing because I didn't set out to make her so beautiful but she refused to be written any other way, which I'm sure owes to the woman who inspired her. However, I failed in making Irina as smart or as interesting as the woman who inspired her, and that woman was, shall we say, a tad upset when she read the manuscript.

Without giving anything away, could you tell us if, in fact, there is an Alexi? And if so, where is he?

I wish I could say he's in Belgrade, but Alexi was kind of a last-minute idea that came to me as a way of trying to close a particular thematic circle. I considered him the riskiest thing I did in the whole book, even though he appears only for a second. But I included him in part *because* of the risk. It seemed cowardly to back away from something that, at least to me, made thematic sense.

Peewee is vivid and memorable. What is it about him, do you think, that makes him so compelling?
I think it's his courage. I mean, here's this tiny guy, but he's got the balls to go against everyone and everything. He's not even afraid to physically take on guys he knows are going to beat the shit out of him. Plus, he's intellectually courageous, even though some of that arises from his considerable contrarian streak.

It's also possible that he stands out because you know from the beginning of the book that he's going to die. So maybe, unconsciously, you think as you're reading, "Oh God, please don't let this happen." I was literally sick with grief when I wrote about the accident. I loved, and love, him so much.

There's a scene in the book where he has a showdown with his father and sinks to the floor in a flood of tears, and you really see, for the first time, the full extent of his damage. I think he suffered terribly. But what does he do? He cries it all out and walks back to Jason and says, "Let's get the fuck out of here." That says everything to me about Peewee. He's a tragic but ballsy little guy.

What is your writing background?
I'm an autodidact. I learned by reading. I was never in a creative writing program or anything like that. I also learned by doing, by writing a lot and poring over what I wrote and studying my mistakes. In terms of professional experience, I've had pieces published in zines and small maga-

zines, that kind of thing. And I've done some screenwriting, and I worked for a number of years on a novel that I ultimately had to scrap. That was a horrible experience, but again, I learned from it, and the lesson was: never, ever write another book told from multiple points of view.

Your sex scenes are... exuberant. How did you approach writing this type of material?

Well, there's one scene that's proven popular with readers, and I have to confess that, in writing it, I thought, "I never read sex scenes that do anything for me, and this one is going to." It was the only moment in the book when I fully surrendered to my inner pornographer, and it must have worked, because I've had male friends, alas, report trips to the bathroom with *Banned* in hand. Also, my friend Jane told me she thought the Jason/Irina relationship was "hot," and that was especially gratifying, not only because it was coming from a woman but because I felt I was holding myself back with those parts.

I don't know. The sex stuff was the same as the music stuff, the same as the Hollywood stuff: I just tried to put myself in a particular place and describe what I felt and saw.

Jason has a strained relationship with his parents. How has your own family reacted to Banned?

They haven't read it. My mom wanted a copy, and I said, "Well, you know, Mom, this book is pretty shocking. Even the first sentence is shocking." And I told her what it was, and she immediately decided this was not a book she preferred to read. I did consider sending a copy to my dad, who I thought would be more open, but my mom said, "Oh, no, your father wouldn't understand that kind of thing at all." Which is a pity because he loves to brag about his kids' accomplishments. I showed

him the manuscript, which he never read, and he would display it to anyone who stopped by: "Here, look what my boy did." But, again, he did
that with no idea what was in it.

How did you celebrate the news Banned *had been picked up by a publisher?*
I didn't, really, because I celebrated the completion of what I thought was
the final draft in 2005 and within days I was rewriting it. Also, Brin Friesen made an offer on behalf of his close friend Dan Starling's imprint,
And/Or Press, following a reading I did with Brin in 2006. It was only
later, after I'd talked to other publishers, that I decided And/Or was the
way to go. The other publishers either wanted to alter the book where I
thought it was unnecessary or they'd shake hands on deals only to renege,
and I trusted Brin, who's a friend and a novelist in his own right. Fortunately, the offer still stood, and the celebration may yet occur. Brin and
I have talked about doing a two-man reading tour, which would include
Vancouver, where And/Or is based. It's only a matter of funds.

In the acknowledgments, Banned *lists some recognizable names. Has there
been any talk among your Hollywood connections of turning the novel into
a film?*
Some talk, yes. It's been kind of a low murmur so far—*very* low. But I do
get the feeling the talk may grow and get louder.

How did you arrive at the title?
Originally the book had a title that now makes me wince. And then
that title was used by somebody else and I was in a great state about it,
and one day I was reading something in, I think, *Spin* magazine about
a band getting banned for life from Holiday Inn—the whole chain—and
I thought, "You know, Banned for Life would make a terrific title." As

I've said, there's a life/death motif that runs throughout the book, along with a big/small motif, among others. So I called a few friends and said, "What do you think?" and everybody seemed to like it, so *Banned for Life* it was.

What's next for you?
Well, I've always been interested in the old physiology-as-destiny idea, in how appearance shapes the way we're regarded and leads to success or the lack of it, and studies have shown that, contrary to widespread belief, men are judged just as much on appearance as women. Also, I tend to write a lot about brothers, which undoubtedly has to do with my having three of them, so I'm working on a new novel concerned with all of the above.

Thanks for "talking" to us!
No, thank *you*. It's my honor to be asked.

GEEZER TALK:
THE TNB SELF-INTERVIEW

The Nervous Breakdown regularly features authors who are asked for an excerpt from their latest published work, as well as a self-interview. D.R. Haney was a featured author in February 2010.

Let's start with a softball question. What's your happiest memory?
I don't think I can point to a single moment as happiest, but there are periods I would cite, like the year I lived in Serbia.

You were famous there.
I was, yeah. I'd acted in a movie entitled *Rat uživo* – *War Live* in English – and there was a lot of publicity for it. I flew back for the premiere, and my first day in Belgrade, I noticed that people on the street were staring at me. I didn't know how much publicity there'd been, so it took me a while to realize why people were staring. I thought, "Did my nose fall off, or did I somehow become incredibly attractive overnight?" Then it dawned on me that I was being *recognized*.

Was it an ego rush?

I'd say it was more a chance to learn how people deal with celebrity from the opposite side of the equation. I remembered making eye contact with celebrities in the past and thinking it meant we had some kind of special rapport, when in fact they were probably wondering if I was staring because I recognized them or if I just found them intriguing without knowing who they were. You always want to think people are interested in you, as opposed to representations of you, so you sometimes find yourself staring back, which, unfortunately, can lead to being approached at moments when you don't much feel like talking.

Was your celebrity part of the reason you liked living in Belgrade?

No. I liked Belgrade because of the friends I'd made while shooting *Rat uživo*, and it was just so extreme to live there. This was during and right after the Milošević period – the Yugoslav wars and all that – and Serbia was estranged from the rest of the world. Plus, I was enamored of this Moscow alt-weekly called *The eXile*, which badly made me want to live in Eastern Europe. I'd always wanted to have that Hemingway expat experience, but in updated terms. I got it with Belgrade, which at the time was kind of like a Slavic Pottersville. You know Pottersville, yes? It's the town in *It's a Wonderful Life* that Bedford Falls *would've* been if Jimmy Stewart had never existed. Well, I much prefer Pottersville to Bedford Falls. Fuck Jimmy Stewart and the goody-two-shoes he walked in on.

And you wrote your novel, Banned for Life, *in Belgrade, right?*

The first draft of it, yes. It was conceived there, in a hotel room one night, which sounds sexual, I know, but I regard *Banned* as my child – a common attitude among writers. Anyway, I'd just finished reading *Get in the Van*, the diary Henry Rollins kept during his Black Flag days, and I thought, "Whatever happened to [Black Flag bass player] Chuck Dukowski?" and suddenly this novel sort of unfolded, based on the premise of a mysteriously vanished punk icon. I saw the book in its entirety, almost, in a minute or less, like an embryo passing through all the stages of gestation at hyperspeed.

So, is Banned *a "thinly disguised memoir," as one review put it?*
It's not. I tried to make it read like one, but despite some biographical overlap, the narrator and I have led very different lives. I was never in a band, for instance. I wanted to be, but it never happened.

Why not?
Well, when I was at the age when most people are forming bands, I was too obsessed with getting my acting career off the ground. Also, I wasn't as crazy about music as I later became. I hung out with musicians—I lived with a number of them—but in many cases I considered seeing bands a chore; something I did to support friends. I felt like if I didn't respond to the music—and I often didn't—I was still forced to stand there and listen. It was like being held prisoner, in a way.

But at some point you changed your mind.
Obviously, yeah. I was bored with making movies and with the cultural climate overall, and I was looking for something that would shake me up and get me excited again, and I realized there was this thriving scene right under my nose. It had always been there, but I'd been too preoccupied to appreciate it. I started going out three and four and five nights a week to see bands, and I learned to play guitar, and lived the life of a musician in every way except by playing in a band. Although I jammed with bands, and friends would put me on the mic at shows. I always delivered, and then some. For instance, two nights before I did my first bookstore reading—Brad Listi, who founded The Nervous Breakdown, read with

me—I closed the show for a band called Memory and completely shredded my voice.

But you got it back in time for the reading.
Just barely, yeah. I had some communication with Greg Olear, who's the author of *Totally Killer*, and his wife, Stephanie, who's a totally killer singer, and Steph advised me on how to recover.

Do you still see a lot of bands?
Not so much. The current music scene is pretty dull, it seems to me. I tend toward heavy, cathartic stuff, and there's not much of it now. I don't think younger audiences are seeking catharsis, which requires an emotional intensity they lack. I realize that's geezer talk, but omnipresent technology is a palliative. Kids are too distracted by all the screens around them, so feelings are experienced dimly, and rock & roll can't cut through the murk. I don't think it's a case of rock & roll being passé; I think contemporary kids are overwhelmingly too passive for rock & roll. They want the karaoke version—the *American Idol* version—when they want it at all.

What about movies? You recently outed yourself, so to speak, as having written the screenplay for—
Don't. Don't mention the name of the movie. I already said everything there is to say about it.

All right. But how would you compare the experience of writing a novel with the experience of writing a screenplay?
They have practically nothing in common, as far as I'm concerned. Prose style doesn't figure in screenwriting. Many people ignore the descriptive bits when they read scripts; they read just the dialogue. Scripts are skimmed, as newspapers have always been skimmed. Close, careful read-

ing of any type of material is, I'm afraid, extinct or moribund, though rule-proving exceptions will naturally survive.

So, you learned nothing at all about writing from working on screenplays?
Well, I'm sure I learned something about storytelling. And I also learned about economy, since you have, with a screenplay, only 120 pages or so in which to do what has to be done. But I probably learned more about writing from acting than I did from working on screenplays.

How so?
It made me more sensitive to character. Acting is like detective work, in a way. You put yourself in a particular place emotionally and report, in a sense, what you find there. It's like: "Well, if I want [another character] to accept my apology, I can't approach her the way the scene's been blocked. I've got to keep my distance." That kind of thing. You're always making these discoveries, and the better the actor, the more astute and refined the discoveries are going to be. Narrative writers have a similar imaginative process, but the majority have never benefited from an acting class. Not that such classes are necessary, but I do think they, and my overall background as an actor, have helped me as a novelist.

Well, in the character department, maybe. But there are other areas—
Yes, and music, for instance, has helped me in writing prose. Rhythm and the sounds of words, the ways they combine—that's everything in shaping a sentence.

And the shape of the narrative?
Well, I'm pretty straightforward in that way. I'm not an innovator. I used to try to be, because I was trained by mentors in the idea that narrative is for idiots, and who cares if the love affair of character A and character B turns out one way or the other? And that attitude hampered me for a

long time because I was so busy trying to be clever in a narrative sense that I was neglecting what I see as my strongest suit, which is portraiture. I demonstrated a talent for visual art from a very young age, and to this day I can draw photorealistically, and the thing I most liked drawing, and painting as well, was people. And acting is an art of portraiture, which is what I now think appealed to me about it, and the novel is likewise an art of portraiture. I mean, you can write a poem without people in it, and there have been novels with animal protagonists – *The Call of the Wild*, for example – but they're anthropomorphized. Now, obviously, you can be innovative with portraiture, but if a portrait is well observed, it's already going to be, if not innovative, then certainly unique.

Do you use real-life models?
I don't tend to use them literally. For instance, Peewee, who's the character most cited in *Banned*, is a hybrid of six different people. That was a conscious choice, but there was also an unconscious element in the way he came about. He was a gift. If we're lucky, we get a great gift every once in a while as writers, and Peewee, for me, was the greatest gift of all. It was like conducting a séance, writing him. I just hope he didn't tap me out in the gift department.

Do you think that's a possibility?
I was really afraid it might be, especially when it took me as long as it did to make a proper start of my next novel. I'd been thinking about the fucking thing for three years, and when I finally sat down to write it, I kept getting stuck. But I think I've got a handle on it now. Not that I have the time to work on it. That's something I'm going to have to buy, and I don't know where, or how, I'm going to come by the money. Fortunately, I don't anticipate it being a lengthy book.

Does it have anything to do with music?
No. I may write about music again—in novel form, I mean—but not the way I did with *Banned*. I was really writing about rebellion with that book, anyway. That's something I should really emphasize when I describe *Banned*. I think people without a background in punk are probably scared off by the idea of reading about it, so maybe I should never mention the word "punk." "What's your book about?" "Oh, rebellion." But, you know, in contemporary America, that's probably a liability, too.

America as in Bedford Falls?
Bedford Falls with TV and computers and cell phones and Kindles, yeah. And Zuzu, the girl with the rose petals, going on *American Idol*.

Do you think Simon Cowell would like her?
Hell, no. "Zuzu, that was *dreadful*. That was the *worst* thing I ever heard. You are *vile*. You are *vomit*."

And how do you think you'd fare?
Oh, for me, they'd roll out the guillotine.

THE GENTLEMAN FROM VIRGINIA: GREG OLEAR CHATS WITH D.R. HANEY

This conversation took place the evening of Thursday, June 3, 2010.

GREG OLEAR: We were recently discussing one of your favorite bands, …And You Shall Know Us by the Trail of Dead, and you were going to tell me how they stumbled upon their economical name.

D.R. HANEY: Well, to be a smartass about it, the name is …And You *Will* Know Us by the Trail of Dead.

OLEAR: What's the difference between "shall" and "will"?

HANEY: Asked like a true English major.

OLEAR: I thought "shall" was more carved-in-stone?

HANEY: Or carved in rock, as it were. Anyway, the band name was originally You Will Know Us by the Trail of Dead, and then they added "…And" so that their name wouldn't always show up last on playlists. *A* instead of *Y*, yes?

OLEAR: The ellipses at the beginning fuck up the alphabetical order, though.

HANEY: Well, you know, I don't really see those guys anymore, or listen to them very much.

OLEAR: Do they have, like, a song that everyone knows, a big hit or something?

HANEY: They never did, no. They never broke out in that way. They were known for their destructive shows. I got hit with a symbol once.

OLEAR: A symbol? Freudian slip.

HANEY: Huh. I'm still pondering that.

OLEAR: Me too. [pauses to drink more beer]

HANEY: I think I hit people with symbols all the time. But don't we all? Anyway, this happened the night before I moved to Serbia. I went to see Trail of the Dead at a place in San Diego called the Casbah.

OLEAR: That's in *Banned*, no? When you went to San Diego to see them play?

HANEY: No, I wrote about a different show in *Banned*. That was the night after I *returned* from Serbia. It seems Serbia was, fittingly, always framed by Trail of the Dead.

OLEAR: Well said.

HANEY: But the show at the Casbah—Jason Reece, the drummer, was destroying his kit, and I got hit with a cymbal, and it fucked up my arm for weeks. I mean, I had a sunset on my arm. But, you know, one wears a bruise like that with pride. I was showing it to all my Serbian friends: "These crazy musicians did this!" They like that kind of thing in Serbia.

OLEAR: I have a book of Eastern European phrases in my desk. I found it while cleaning out the shed. [reads] "*Imate li upaljac.*"

HANEY: I only remember the curse words.

OLEAR: Those are not in this fucking book. I speak French a bit, and when we were in France, it irritated me to no end that I couldn't swear. It was like having one less finger or something. Quite a disability.

HANEY: I know how to swear in French. I can proudly swear in a number of languages.

OLEAR: So, band names. How did you come up with the band names in *Banned*?

HANEY: Actually, one of the first things I did when I had the idea for *Banned* was to make lists of band names. Of course I'm *always* coming up with imaginary band names. Anyway, I made lists and lists and showed them to people, and they said, "Oh, I really like Rule of Thumb." Which I had to admit was the best name I'd come up with.

OLEAR: Yes. And the abbreviation is ROT, which is perfect.

HANEY: Yeah, that was a happy byproduct. And then, for the names of Jason and Peewee's bands, I went with something cheesy for the first one, which is the Widowmakers. I mean, Jason and Peewee were kids when they started the Widowmakers. And then Scratch was something that later came to me, and the Egonauts was a sudden inspiration, and from there it was an easy jump to Superego, which is the name of Jason and Peewee's last band. I was thinking of Superchunk with that one.

OLEAR: The Egonauts, as in Jason and the… Very clever, that one.

HANEY: Yes, well, that was Peewee being a jerk. He and Jason were on the outs at the time, and Peewee named his new band as a way of taunting Jason.

OLEAR: You wrote the lyrics of all the Rule of Thumb songs mentioned in *Banned*. How did you do that? Was there music in your head? Are there recordings stashed away somewhere?

HANEY: Well, I felt that, since I couldn't include a CD with the book, I should nonetheless put the sound of the band – all of the bands – in the reader's head, and one way to do that, I thought, was to write lyrics. But lyrics are very hard to write. Those bits were some of the hardest in the entire book, because lyrics are just so fucking hard to write well.

OLEAR: "Banished" is particularly good.

HANEY: Yeah, and guess what? That was the only lyrical bit that came to me in an instant. The others required a lot of labor. I didn't want the characters to sound stupid, and that's such an easy outcome with lyrics. I mean, Paul McCartney still writes stupid lyrics. You'd think he'd avoid easy rhymes by now, but he doesn't.

OLEAR: The Beatles were lousy lyricists in general. They are way overrated in that regard.

HANEY: Well, the standards weren't high when the Beatles first appeared. Dylan had just started to raise them. I think you get some great lyrics with the Beatles later. "A Day in the Life," for instance, is good that way, or the John bits are.

OLEAR: "Back in the USSR" is pretty funny.

HANEY: Yeah, they were great with satire. That's a very funny song.

OLEAR: I think the John part of "A Day in the Life" is an A+, but the Paul section is a C+. It makes for an uneven listening experience: "Dragged a comb across my head…" Ugh.

HANEY: Yeah, but I like that they took bits from two songs and melded them. Also, are there any guys who use combs anymore? I was thinking about that recently. In the sixties, I think guys carried combs with them everywhere.

OLEAR: Nowadays, bedhead is the thing. Hipsters just roll out of bed. The comb is verboten.

HANEY: True.

OLEAR: But back to the Beatles: they included the high-pitched squeals at the end, to rouse the dogs. Pet sounds. Get it?

HANEY: Are you talking about "Good Morning" on *Sgt. Pepper*? I hadn't considered that before, but you're probably right.

OLEAR: It's absolutely done for that reason: to drive Brian Wilson insane.

HANEY: I like the way bands interacted in those days. They were always trying to top each other, but usually in a friendly way. That's how "Helter Skelter" came to be written: Paul read somewhere that the Who had written the most explosive rock & roll song ever, and Paul thought, "No, *I'm* going to write the most explosive rock & roll song ever."

OLEAR: I have a friend who was a metalhead in high school, who insists that "Helter Skelter" is the first metal song. Paul McCartney, of all people, invented heavy metal.

HANEY: I don't know that McCartney invented metal, but he helped to invent punk, oddly enough. Thurston Moore of Sonic Youth once said that there'd be no Sonic Youth without "Helter Skelter." Which, when you listen to "Helter Skelter," makes perfect sense. It really does kind of sound like Sonic Youth.

OLEAR: I like that the Beatles met Bob Dylan, wrote "Hide Your Love Away," a "Bob Dylan song" that is superior to anything Dylan ever produced, and then moved on. Game, set, match.

HANEY: Well, musically, "You've Got to Hide Your Love Away" is great, but the Beatles never topped Dylan lyrically. Also, I'll take "Positively 4th Street" over almost anything the Beatles ever did. That's a tremendous song in every conceivable way.

OLEAR: I never got into Dylan, I think because my first exposure to him was – don't laugh – in the video for "We Are the World," and he's *awful* in that.

HANEY: Yeah, but it's such an awful song. I don't think anyone came out looking good there.

OLEAR: Oh, come. "*There comes a time,*" Duke, "*when we heed a certain call. When you're down and out, there seems no hope at all!*"

HANEY: Did Paul McCartney write those lyrics?

OLEAR: Ha! Legend has it that Michael Jackson wrote and recorded most of it in one marathon all-nighter.

HANEY: You know what strikes me about so much music from the eighties? How a song starts out about one thing and at some point it turns into "Let's dance!" I mean, it could be about killing your father, you know, but suddenly the chorus is "Move your body! Feel the beat! Let's boogie all night!"

OLEAR: Well, you know, if you feel it, you gotta shake it. Speaking of the eighties: man, I hated how "The Reflex" was playing during the crash that killed Peewee. I was actually like, "No! Not that!"

HANEY: We've discussed this before, but it hasn't done anything to change my position. I still think "The Reflex" is about as bad as bad gets.

OLEAR: We agree to disagree.

HANEY: The funny thing is, Die Princess Die used to be called the Reflex, in homage to that song.

OLEAR: It's about masturbation, you know. *"Try not to bruise it."*

HANEY: I didn't know.

OLEAR: *"I'm on a ride and I wanna get off."*

HANEY: I'm confused. Does this mean that Simon Le Bon was making excursions off the highway to jerk off?

OLEAR: I have no clue.

HANEY: One hopes that wasn't the case.

OLEAR: All I know is, Simon has a book blog, and I sent him a galley of *Totally Killer*, and he never read it.

HANEY: Well, that tells you everything you need to know, I suppose.

OLEAR: Seriously. He has a book blog.

HANEY: Where he reviews—what?—*The DaVinci Code*?

OLEAR: That's one of the books he discusses, I'm ashamed to admit. I can't say anything bad about Simon. I just can't.

HANEY: That's okay. I'll do it for you.

OLEAR: One critic complained, idiotically in my view, that *Banned* is a "thinly veiled memoir." It sounds like one, but of course it isn't. Which character in your book is the closest to the real-life Duke Haney?

HANEY: I think Jason [Maddox, the narrator in *Banned*] *sounds* the most like me. But I'm weirder and artier than Jason, so in that way I'm closer to Peewee, and I think some of my bitterness comes out through Jim.

OLEAR: While writing, did you find yourself at the point where Jason starts out being you and then deviates? I love when that happens.

HANEY: I don't think he deviated significantly. No, he came out pretty much as I expected. Peewee was the big surprise. He was the most delightful character to write, and I think it shows.

OLEAR: Jason is quite the lothario. I remember a passage where he says he's slept with, what, eighty women or something, and he doesn't find that to be a high number. Which brings us to a prepared question: the other day when we spoke, you were talking about Jason and you said that there seemed to be a dearth of, for want of a better word, macho characters in literary fiction. "If I have to read one more novel about a fucking college professor," you began. Complete that thought.

HANEY: Well, I don't know that I said "macho." I think I said "masculine." Macho guys are usually assholes, as we know.

OLEAR: Right. I knew I'd gotten that wrong. I wish I wrote down what you said. It was really compelling.

HANEY: It doesn't matter. I'm flattered that you remember what I said at all. But I wasn't trying to say that a professor can't be masculine. What I was getting at was that masculine characters don't appear much in contemporary literary fiction, and I was trying to redress that imbalance in *Banned*.

OLEAR: I've always thought your stuff reminds me of Henry Miller, who is, of course, quite masculine.

HANEY: Thank you. I'm flattered. Yes, I'll take that.

OLEAR: I love Henry Miller. He's not read much these days. The opening of *Tropic of Cancer* can stand with anything. You can feel how vital he is. *Banned* has the same quality, and I think *Subversia* reads like Miller, who wasn't really writing fiction, per se.

HANEY: Well, except that I hardly wrote about sex in *Subversia*.

OLEAR: True, but there's plenty of it in *Banned*. And, my God, some of Miller's passages are insane in that regard.

HANEY: I tend to write about sex in the guise of fiction. It's ungentlemanly to fuck and tell. I am from Virginia, you know. We're all raised to be gentlemen in Virginia.

OLEAR: Now, that's a good song lyric: "We're all raised to be gentlemen in Virginia." And at the end of the song, we discover that Virginia is a woman, not a state.

HANEY: Ha! But it comes to me now that when we were having that talk about masculinity and the way it's portrayed these days, I said that when Colin Farrell first appeared, I kept seeing articles everywhere that were like "He drinks! He smokes! He gets laid!" And I thought, "Well, so does every guy I know." Journalists were acting like it was this shocking thing, and it wasn't. But maybe if you live in an ivory-tower sort of world it really is.

OLEAR: The Serb men sure seem to be masculine. That's their rap, anyway. Are the Serbs bellicose people?

HANEY: Well, they certainly pride themselves on being warriors. They were invaded again and again for centuries.

OLEAR: By the Croats?

HANEY: By everyone: the Romans, the Nazis, the Ottomans. The Ottomans are the ones they're still pissed about.

OLEAR: Yeah, the Ottomans were not so nice.

HANEY: There's a wall in the town of Niš that's made up of skulls. The Ottomans were pissed about pockets of resistance, and they lined up hundreds of people and beheaded them and made a wall of the heads to stand as a warning to the resistance.

OLEAR: Now, *that's* what I call an art installation. I've seen pictures of Serbia, and it doesn't look like a place I'd want to visit, let alone live. Yet Serbia was inspirational for you.

HANEY: Well, first of all, parts of it are very beautiful.

OLEAR: Parts of Queens are beautiful. Parts of Newark are beautiful.

HANEY: Yeah, but I've never seen mountains like the ones I did in Serbia. It's something. But I'll admit that Belgrade is ugly. It was the people I loved. They were just very hospitable and fun-loving and always ready for trouble of a kind I like.

OLEAR: What kind of trouble do you like?

HANEY: Oh, it's very predictable, I think.

OLEAR: Sex, drugs, rock & roll?

HANEY: Yeah. There were tons of drugs in Belgrade, and I like drugs. I've never had a bad experience on drugs, except for alcohol, and that, iron-ically, is legal.

OLEAR: What kind of drugs do you like? Sudafed? NyQuil?

HANEY: Rimshot! No, heroin is my favorite. But I only dabbled. I wasn't about to fuck up my life by becoming a junkie, so I was careful to limit my dealings.

OLEAR: Good thing. You get too addicted to smack, you wind up writing a song like "Captain Jack." Do you know that song?

HANEY: No.

OLEAR: I didn't think so.

HANEY: Who's it by?

OLEAR: I'm too ashamed to tell you. The last name rhymes with "foal" and the first name with "silly."

HANEY: Your shame is now understood.

OLEAR: One of my earliest pieces at The Nervous Breakdown was about him.

HANEY: About Silly Foal?

OLEAR: Yes. I must say, he hasn't aged well. His body or his music.

HANEY: Yeah, he looks like the troll he probably always was. I saw him interviewed on TV a few years ago, and he was kind of nasty. But, you know, as we get older, we become more who we really are, I think, and it shows more in our appearance. I'm sure this explains my own monstrousness.

OLEAR: You have an iconic look, I'd say. Not at all monstrous. You look cooler than you think you do. There aren't many people in L.A. who dress like you do. You have a more New York look, I'd say. Are you trying to cultivate a look?

HANEY: I kind of feel like my options are limited, dress-wise. It comes down to poverty, in part.

OLEAR: Yes, clothes are expensive.

HANEY: Also, I slowly started to realize that I prefer clothes that look like uniforms. I dress like a security guard. Which is a job I used to have.

OLEAR: Where did you do that?

HANEY: At Hunter College, as per Jason in *Banned*. And I was fired for a similar reason.

OLEAR: Did you live on the Upper East Side? I know the German bar off 86th Street you mention in *Banned*. The Heidelberg.

HANEY: Oh, the Heidelrock. That's what my roommates used to call it.

OLEAR: Why?

HANEY: It's a reference to *The Flintstones*, where everything always has the word "rock" in it. Anyway, yeah, I lived right above the Heidelrock. I was drunk around the clock.

OLEAR: Do you prefer Wilma or Betty?

HANEY: I always preferred Wilma, which puts me in the minority, I know. But I like her red hair with the bone in it. It's that fiery, carnivorous thing.

OLEAR: I think I'm also a Wilma man. The bone is rather suggestive. But I don't really dig on cavewomen.

HANEY: Well, the hygiene couldn't have been ideal. And I was once madly in love with this girl, and I said to her, "Wouldn't it be great if we were savages?" and she said, "Yeah, and then I could die from an abscessed tooth." She had a good point there, even though I knew then it probably would never work out.

OLEAR: So, what's your favorite drink? If I were to buy you one, what would it be?

HANEY: Jameson.

OLEAR: I drink that, too. Usually with soda.

HANEY: Actually, I think I'd go for a boilermaker. Did you ever see *A River Runs Through It*?

OLEAR: No, but I just wrote an article on fly-fishing. Also: "boilermaker" is the best drink name ever.

HANEY: Well, there's a scene where Brad Pitt and Craig Sheffer, who play brothers, order boilermakers. They get mugs of beer and drop shot glasses of whisky into the mugs and drink the beer until the shot glasses are right up against their mouths and they're gripping them with their teeth. I thought, "Now, *that's* the way to drink a fucking boilermaker!"

OLEAR: I have to try that. But not, you know, right now.

HANEY: I think you should. I'll wait. Hey, do you want to discuss some of the pieces in *Subversia*?

OLEAR: Have I read them? Kidding.

HANEY: You haven't read the new ones. Well, no, there's just one new piece you haven't read. But you read the one about James Dean.

OLEAR: Yes, that and "Sunset on Sunset," which is terrific. I'm afraid I sound like a fucking game-show host when I talk about your stuff. I'm not this complimentary to everyone.

HANEY: I know. We'll have to leave time at the end of the interview for you to slam a few people.

OLEAR: What's your own favorite piece in the book?

HANEY: Actually, I like the one about Dean quite a bit. I showed it to Jake, who's mentioned in the piece, and he was really enthusiastic about it. I was afraid he wouldn't be, since he might not like the way he was represented, but that thankfully wasn't the case. And we were both good friends with Paul, and we talked about how sad we were that things worked out as they did with him. But I think "The Worst Crime" is probably the best thing I ever put up at TNB.

OLEAR: I agree. It's the last piece you did chronologically, and it book-ends well with your first piece, which concerns the suicidal Elliott Smith.

HANEY: Yeah, "The Worst Crime" was a weird one, because I started it a long time before I finished, which isn't how it usually is with my stuff at TNB. I was in a black mood one night, and I started writing about suicide, and then I put the piece down for a few weeks. And then I decided to incorporate Kurt Cobain, and I finally had this inspiration about how to finish, months later.

OLEAR: Inspired by Jim Morrison, who isn't alluded to at all in the piece.

HANEY: Yeah, it was seeing that documentary about the Doors, *When You're Strange*, that made it all come together. I realized, watching Jim Morrison, what's missing in my life so much of the time, which is passion.

OLEAR: Odd, as your work is so infused with passion. *Banned* is all about passion. That's what makes it so inspiring.

HANEY: Yeah, and that goes back to the lothario thing. I mean, that's another reason I wanted Jason to be a bit of a lothario. I wanted him to be a passionate guy.

OLEAR: Is D.R. Haney a lothario?

HANEY: I'd say I'm more of a retired lothario. I no longer have the looks to pull it off. Just like I'm no longer the king of the TNB comment boards.

OLEAR: You're the Wayne Gretzky of the comment boards! Check Gretzky's stats. No one touches that guy.

HANEY: I've since been supplanted by one Greg Olear.

OLEAR: I only get a lot of comments when I talk about you in some way.

HANEY: Well, yeah, I was once a king.

OLEAR: Past tense? Others may beg to differ.

HANEY: Let them beg. That sounds kind of kingly, huh?

OLEAR: I'd say you revolutionized the comment board, which consequently revolutionized the site. You made it more of a social club. Without you, I don't know if it happens the way it did.

HANEY: I never meant for that to happen at all. I think, if it's more of a social site now and I had something to do with that, it was probably a mistake. TNB may be *too* clubby at this point. But I was just being myself. I'm talkative, as you well know. Except when I'm not. I'm very withdrawn at times. I can go for days without speaking to anybody.

OLEAR: You once got in trouble on the comment boards with a certain Playmate of the Month. What did you call her? A sociopathic cunt?

HANEY: It wasn't quite that bad. I only use the c-word with guys, which doesn't offend the way it does when it's applied to women. But, yeah, with my male friends, I'll say, "You fucking cunt."

OLEAR: That's very British of you. As is the word "kingly."

HANEY: Well, my ancestry is completely British. I'm English, Irish, and Scottish all the way. It's ironic that I dis Brits in *Banned*.

OLEAR: Out with it, Duke. Which Playmate was it?

HANEY: Please, no names. But here's what happened. Lenore Zion, who's one of my favorite TNB contributors and one of my favorite people, wrote a piece about lying, and I commented about the biggest lies I ever told, and one of them was about a certain Playmate.

OLEAR: Could it be that she's the mother of someone famous?

HANEY: Stop it, Greg!

OLEAR: Does her name not have the same rhythm as "Don't Be Cruel"?

HANEY: Put the beer down! Anyway, when I was a kid, I had a crush on this Playmate, and I told friends I'd written her a letter and she called me.

OLEAR: But she didn't. Playmates don't meet guys that way.

HANEY: Especially when the guys are twelve. Like I say, Lenore's piece was about lying, and my comment had to do with the biggest lies I ever told. So Lenore came back with "Which Playmate was it?" And I mentioned her name, and Lenore wrote, "Oh, I know who that is. She's really pretty." And I wrote, "Yeah, but she's a sociopathic whore," hoping to make Lenore laugh. I have a brutal sense of humor, and so does Lenore sometimes, and I thought she'd get a kick out of it.

OLEAR: "Whore," that's not so bad. Just an innocuous comment, way down the comment board.

HANEY: Exactly. And the very next day, I check my e-mail, and there's a message saying the Playmate had sent me a message at MySpace. I thought, "Well, that's weird. I just wrote a comment about her on TNB yesterday. You don't think…"

OLEAR: Oh, brother.

HANEY: Yeah. She'd read the fucking comment, and wrote, "A friend brought this to my attention," as if she hadn't been sitting there Googling herself. And she went on with: "How dare you say that! Do I even know you?" So I apologized and asked Lenore to remove the comment, which she did, and I wrote again to the Playmate to apologize, and she wrote back with: "I've had stalkers! It's scary when people say that kind of thing!"

OLEAR: I'm sorry, Miss November. I can't hear you over the screech of the violins.

HANEY: The funny thing is, she made my lie a truth. I'd finally had contact with her.

OLEAR: In your face, Charlottesville middle-schoolers!

HANEY: Yeah. "One day I *will* speak to her! I'll call her a sociopathic whore, and she'll write me an angry message on technology that hasn't been invented yet!"

OLEAR: This might be a good moment to wrap up. My wife is snoring.

HANEY: Okay, well. I'll let you go to bed, you drunk.

OLEAR: Ha! I rarely drink, and almost never at home.

HANEY: I'm the opposite. I drink all the time, and almost *always* at home. I can't afford to drink at bars.

OLEAR: Sleep tight. I'm off.

HANEY: Me too. I'm *very* off.

ACKNOWLEDGMENTS

SOME TIME AGO, my friend Sarah Paradoski, now of St. Louis but then of Brooklyn, started a blog called Irresponsiville. I regarded "Irresponsiville" as the greatest name ever, and I set out to coin a similar name for a blog of my own. "Subversia" was the result, and when I mentioned it to Sarah, she said, "Subversia sounds like it could be a neighborhood in Irresponsiville." The blog I had in mind would focus on rebellious figures – Byron in one entry, Eddie Cochran in another – but it never materialized. Instead, to state the obvious, *Subversia* became the title of a book, and I'd like to publicly credit Sarah for inspiring it.

Originally, this book had a different title, but Greg Olear suggested *Subversia* as more in keeping with the book's spirit. Greg acted as my unofficial editor, helping to sequence the selected pieces, and I'm grateful on that account, as well as for Greg's foreword and the time he generously donated in ways too numerous to list.

While designing the book, Charlotte Howard and Jeannie Hart were patient to the point of saintliness, always prepared to accommodate new ideas and quick to respond to anxious messages about this detail or that one. Ben Loory's input on the cover art was invaluable, as was the input of Lenore Zion, while Chris Gage scrupulously copyedited the manuscript and galleys, spotting errors no one else had noticed. Heather Mills D'Augustine, Joe D'Augustine, and Rachel Pollon Williams provided crucial feedback as the book was being finalized.

The *Subversia* iPad edition includes a documentary, *How I Became Human*, which was directed by the talented Timothy Murray. A number of bands, singers, and record labels permitted their music to be used in *How I Became Human*, and I'm indebted in every instance, just as I'm indebted to everyone who provided blurbs and photographs. My mother, Sara Matthews, intrepidly dug through myriad boxes full of old photographs and forwarded the results, so I'd like to offer special thanks in her case.

I'd also like to thank Joseph Matheny of Hukilau for his labor on the *Subversia* e-book editions, as well as for his expertise in all matters technical and otherwise. Joe is a contributor to The Nervous Breakdown, as is Megan Power, who signed off on the inclusion of her interview with me: my first as a novelist. I wish I had space enough to individually thank every TNB contributor, to say nothing of the friends and relatives who've provided so much love and support. You know who you are, and if I haven't said so lately: you're the best.

Finally, and most importantly, I hereby lift a toast to the founder of The Nervous Breakdown. It was his idea to collect my TNB pieces and publish them as the inaugural title at TNB Books, and he worked his ass off to see the project through.

So here's to you, Brad Listi. A refill? Of course. The drinks are on me, and that goes for every person cited above, whether by name or not.

D.R. HANEY was born in Virginia and moved in his teens to New York City, where he studied acting, and later to Los Angeles, where he supported himself as a screenwriter. In 2009, he published *Banned for Life*, a novel about punk rock, and he is presently at work on a novel tentatively entitled *A Perfect Example*.

LaVergne, TN USA
29 September 2010
198873LV00001B/41/P